WORLD WAR II
ARROYO GRANDE

···

JIM GREGORY

THE
History
PRESS

Published by The History Press
Charleston, SC
www.historypress.net

First published 2016

Manufactured in the United States

ISBN 978.1.46711.958.0

Library of Congress Control Number: 2015955228

For Joseph Ira Loomis and James H. Hayes, no better friends, no finer men

And in gratitude for the gift of my mother, Patricia Margaret Keefe Gregory,
1921–1969

CONTENTS

ACKNOWLEDGEMENTS

This book would not have been possible without the support and immense patience of my wife, Elizabeth, who spent months with a husband who was gone, not to faraway places, but to places in the past—lost on Branch Street in 1937 or under machine-gun fire in a Norman farm field.

Profuse and heartfelt thanks go to the inspiration of my Cal Poly history professor, Dan Krieger, and his wife, Liz, who are unparalleled experts on San Luis Obispo County history; to my longtime English teaching partner, Amber Derbidge, for proofreading the first draft; to the South County Historical Society's Ross Kongable and Joe Swigert; to South County historians Linda Austin, Effie McDermott and Shirley Bennett Gibson; to friends like Mary Giambalvo and Gerrie Quaresma; and to new friends, like Manetta Bennett, who is a joy to know. From Cal Poly–San Luis Obispo, my thanks go to Dr. Grace Yeh, whose studies of the work and the lives of local immigrants sometimes cross the line from academics into poetry, and to Laura Sorvetti and the staff at Poly's Special Collections and Archives Library, who were incredibly supportive. Gary Nakamura shared his father's story with great grace. Longtime friends like the Fuchiwakis, Silvas, Shannons, Kobaras, Loomises, Alarcios and Ikedas were generous in sharing their families' histories. Jennifer Silva was a thorough and valuable help in researching local servicemen and women. It was a particular pleasure to interview Mr. Haruo Hayashi, the epitome of what my Irish American mother raised me to be: a gentleman.

Special thanks to three extraordinary people who have graced my life: My high school friend Joe Loomis inherited the innate sense of generosity that so marks his family, and I have never had a more genuine friend. Jim Hayes, a Cal Poly journalism professor and a copy editor when I was a newspaper reporter, was a stern taskmaster who struck terror and sparks at his copy desk but could never quite disguise the depth of his kindness and wisdom. My mother, whose ancestors escaped famine poverty in County Wicklow, grew up poor, and though I still do not understand how she did it, she was able to push aside the insecurity of her own childhood and teach her four children lessons—so deep they might have been engraved—in charity, responsibility and justice. She remains the most remarkable person I've ever known.

All of these people believe, as I do, that history is alive, that it surrounds and shapes us every day and that we all owe a great debt to those who not only inhabit the past but, in some important ways, still live with us in the present.

INHERITANCE

This is the history of a small California farm town and its role in the greatest and most destructive conflict in human history. Arroyo Grande lies along the coast, about midway between Los Angeles and San Francisco, and like any American town, its character has been shaped by immigrants from distant places.

So, this is a story that's a little like Exodus: its characters will enter the Arroyo Grande Valley, many after long and dangerous journeys; World War II will call their descendants—part of "the Greatest Generation"—away on journeys more dangerous still; and with war's end, those young people will come home to resume the journeys of their lives in a manner that ennobles them.

I began this book during my last year in the classroom and finished it in retirement. I taught history for thirty years, and I never, never ceased to get angry every spring when I taught the First World War. It was this war and its peace treaty that did so much to make World War II possible. In 2010, I took some of my students to Western Europe's World War II battlefields but also to Verdun, site of a horrific 1916 battle that lasted over ten months. The stacked bones in the ossuary there once belonged to boys like my two sons, whose parents had applauded at their first steps or cheered when they scored their first football goal.

I made it my business to help all of my students understand that idea—that war cheats us all so cruelly—and so I led them, every year in my classroom, into dark places, like Fort Douaumont at Verdun, so dark that it swallowed the light of five hundred years of Western culture. To go inside Douaumont,

Branch Street, Arroyo Grande. *Author photo.*

where 100,000 young men were killed or wounded, to study war doesn't mean we glorify it. A few years ago, a student told me the First World War was her favorite unit. (Not mine—I much prefer *La Belle Èpoque.*) I asked her why, and she replied, "Now I understand how precious human life is."

She understood precisely why I became a history teacher.

She would have understood, as well, how in the process of writing this book, something extraordinary has happened within my heart: the more I research these young men of my father's generation, the inheritors of the legacy of places like Douaumont, the more they become my sons.

Through no one's fault, they've been mostly forgotten. This book seeks to name them and so reclaim them for a new generation. When we come to know these young men, we come to love them, and maybe that is the force that will carry us a small step farther along a path that will lead us to a world of peace. The great Jesuit theologian and anthropologist Pierre Teilhard de Chardin believed that we have a divine gift. We evolve physically and intellectually, but, he argued, we can evolve spiritually, as well. I believe Teilhard is exactly right. But I believe also that we cannot advance if we leave behind the boys and men I've met, the casualties of war. Their lives were, and are, precious, and if they could somehow save other young lives, I think they'd do it in an instant.

A North Vietnamese soldier-poet wrote many years ago that "the bullet that kills a soldier passes first through his mother's heart." If the young men I now know could somehow spare other mothers the pain theirs went through, then I think they would do that in an instant, too.

It is our responsibility to confront and understand the horrific violence that took their lives. The young men I now know who died in a Norman village like Le Bot or in the sky over the English Channel or deep in the waters of Ironbottom Sound off Guadalcanal lit a path, in dying, for the living to follow. If we ignore them, we will lose the path, and the dark will have won after all.

These young men would have known intimately the world like the one outside my boyhood bedroom window in the Upper Arroyo Grande Valley, where at night I could hear the click of train wheels near the surf line of the Pacific Ocean, four miles away, as freight cars picked up speed to carry valley produce from packing sheds to distant markets.

Those sounds belonged to the Lower Valley, where fields of row crops, soft greens—and, if cabbage is in, blues—abruptly end at epic sand dunes

The upper Arroyo Grande Valley shows evidence of two activities that have marked its history: a cattle trough on the hillside and fields of row crops beyond. *Author photo.*

along the sea. Tucked into a narrowing between the Upper and Lower Valleys is the town of Arroyo Grande, whose Branch Street is flanked by narrow storefronts, some brick, some fronted by Victorian gingerbread façades. Sometimes, even today, automobile traffic will slow because of tractor traffic. It was, and is, a farm town, and locals wince when travel magazines invariably use the adjective "quaint" to insult it.

Just east of Old Arroyo, farm fields also bordered the house where I grew up during the 1950s and 1960s. With my big brother, I walked through them on my way to school, past men cultivating crops with *el cortito*, the "short hoe"—backbreaking work with a tool that would be outlawed in 1974. The soil of these fields is rich and loamy, alluvial deposits that are the gift of the Arroyo Grande Creek, which flows into the Pacific Ocean seven miles from its origins in the Santa Lucia Mountains.

During my childhood, the creek was my playground. My friends and I fished for rainbow trout in little eddies and in a beaver pond adjacent to farmer Kazuo Ikeda's cabbages. In fact, steelhead trout still swam upstream to spawn; they are now gone this far south in California. I hooked one once when I was eleven, and the shock of the big fish hitting and then fighting made me nearly drop my pole. I had never seen anything quite so beautiful and so violent—so determined to escape and to live. She did both.

It was earning a living that absorbed my father; a brilliant man with a gift for numbers, he became an accountant who was determined that his children would not suffer anything like the poverty he'd seen among his neighbors in the Ozark foothills during the Great Depression. Beyond that, he was determined that they would all get a college education. His mother, our grandmother Gregory, had been a rural schoolmarm. My education began with two severe but gifted women at the two-room Branch Elementary School, another rural school, with some seventy-odd students in grades one through eight.

Though our teachers dressed like the women in Grant Woods's *Daughters of the American Revolution*, they had none of the insipid smugness of Wood's subjects. These women were teachers because they had the calling; their lives had purpose. Each had to choreograph teaching six subjects to four grades—first through fourth in one room, fifth through eighth in the other—and so they ran a tight ship. We would learn *their* way, a requirement for which, many years later, I would be deeply grateful.

My first teacher, however, was my mother, and she was remarkable. Her childhood had been a hard one. She grew up poor. Her ne'er-do-well Irish father deserted the family when she was a toddler in an oil boomtown, Taft,

Above: Branch Elementary school is today a private residence. *Author photo.*

Right: Patricia Keefe Gregory, my mother, with my sister, Roberta, 1943. *Author's collection.*

just over the county line. When I was very little, we played school. She even rang a hand bell—it had been Grandmother Gregory's—when "recess" was over. On my first day of formal education, I remember realizing, with a little shock of pleasure, that I could read the names of my classmates as our teacher, Mrs. Brown, wrote them on the blackboard.

One lesson appeared to my mother in the form of a Mexican fieldworker, a *bracero*, who one day walked into our front yard and up to her. She kept her garden shears at port arms and shoved me behind her skirts. The man signaled that he wanted to fill an empty wine gallon jug with water for himself and his friends, who were working the pepper field adjacent to our pasture. His face, with a tiny Cantínflas mustache, radiated good humor. My

Farmer and neighbor George Shannon, with his middle son, Jerry. *Photo courtesy Michael Shannon.*

mother relaxed and filled the jug from her garden hose. The water was cold. I knew that because of what she said next.

"Now, help him carry it back."

So I did. And I stayed awhile. These men worked for George Shannon, a man of immense warmth, and on later visits to their barracks at Shannon's farm—it smelled of earth and Aqua Velva and laundry soap—I learned a little Spanish from the *braceros*. They spread snapshots across their bunks of wives and girlfriends and children, and they laughed when I tried out my new words in their language. That encounter would lead to my college studies' focus, the history of Mexico and Latin America, but the valley and its people—people who were Mexicans and Mexican American and the sons and daughters of immigrants from the Azores, Japan and the Philippines—educated me, as well.

I met this second generation when I was a little boy, when they had started families of their own; they were the contemporaries of my parents. But before I came to know them, their lives had been interrupted by the costliest and most dramatic conflict of modern times. They suffered deprivation, heartbreak and injustice, and finally, they celebrated victory. The celebration was brief. There were family relationships to be rebuilt, friendships to rekindle and there were deep hurts that would need time to heal, hurts inflicted all the way from the hedgerows of Normandy to the desolate, shell-blasted landscape of Iwo Jima and the now empty baseball fields in internment camps like Gila River.

There were crops to be brought in, and there were lives to be lived.

PART I

DISTANT FIELDS

· ·

CHAPTER 1

SUMMER 1944

In the early summer of 1944—when Eisenhower pauses at the end of his weather officer's report for June 6 and says simply, "OK, we'll go," when Rome falls to Mark Clark's armies and when horrified marines watch Japanese civilians leap to their deaths from the cliffs of Saipan—the war, for Americans at home, was both distant and, for grieving families, painfully intimate, but even the war could not touch the work to be done.

That month, in the upper Arroyo Grande Valley of coastal California, this is what you would see, possibly through the dense, cold morning fog: labor contractors drop off pickup loads of fieldworkers at the Harris Bridge, which spans the creek that nourishes and gives the valley its name.

The workers cross the bridge whistling, an incredibly beautiful, almost baroque whistling of Mexican folk tunes from the time of the revolution or love songs, as they walk down to the fields to their work with their lunches—wine jugs filled with drinking water and perhaps chorizo-and-egg burritos wrapped in wax paper, fuel for the kind of physical work that would make most men sit in the freshly turned field gasping within fifteen minutes and woefully regarding their quickly blistered hands.

Their summer work might be in a new bean field, where the whistling would eventually stop because it is such a tax on men who work hard, whose breathing soon becomes laborious and therefore precious. To begin a newly planted field of beans, the fieldworkers have to drive wooden stakes into precise parade-ground lines along the furrows, so that the bean vines can use the stakes to climb and twist—they will eventually bear delicate,

Row crops alongside Huasna Road, Upper Arroyo Grande Valley. The valley's first settler, Francis Branch, built his adobe home on the bare knoll in the distance. *Author photo.*

bell-shaped flowers—as they stretch toward the sun. The sun invariably appears in late morning, when it burns the sea fog away, and the colors of the valley—wheaten hills and verdant bottomland where the crop is in— are reborn, vivid and sharply focused.

To drive the wooden stakes, the fieldworkers use a heavy metal tube, a driver, with a handle attached that resembles that of an old-time pump primer that nineteenth-century settlers used to draw water from the ground. So the whistling stops and is replaced by the rhythmic ring of the stake drivers as the workers pound hundreds of stakes into the field.

It is a musical sound. But of course, what you cannot hear are the grunts of the men at each stroke of the stake driver; what you cannot feel is the enormous weight that exhausted arms and shoulders soon take on; and what you cannot avoid, if you think about it sensibly, is admiration for the men who feed you. In turn, they are determined to feed families who live in camps or tarpaper shacks in the valley or, for part of the workforce who will dominate agriculture here for the next twenty years, who live in the states of northern and central Mexico.

It is these men who are working the fields in 1944. Four years before, many of the laborers would have been Filipino or Japanese, but they are gone now—many Filipinos are in transit to New Guinea to join MacArthur's forces in the Southwest Pacific, where they are preparing to retake the Philippines; the Japanese have been exiled to bleak, arid internment camps.

As the war began to wind down, the Japanese began to come home. The Kobara family, whose patriarch was jailed the day after the Pearl Harbor attack, will be the first. But many, many families—their children leave unfamiliar surnames in prewar high school yearbooks—will never come home. The hurt was too deep.

Yet years after the war and internment, Japanese American farmers—like the Kobaras, the Ikedas, the Hayashis—are integral to Arroyo Grande. Agriculture has changed—pole beans and the seemingly limitless groves of walnut trees that once competed with row crops are gone, the latter victims of a malevolent infestation of insect larvae. Today, farmers grow more exotic crops, like bok choy and kale, and along the hillsides given over to beef cattle as far back as the beginning of the nineteenth century, there are new farmers and new rows of wine grapes, profitable, lovely and greedy for water—a commodity that isn't plentiful in California—multiplying every year. The beef cattle haven't dominated the coastal hills since the 1860s, when the drought that periodically afflicts the state hit as hard as it ever has. The cattle, either killed outright by ravenous coyotes or mountain lions come down from distant folds in the hills or dead of thirst and hunger, would have covered the hills with their bones.

It was that kind of drought that may have brought a fieldworker, whose family had lived for generations in New Mexico, to these coastal valleys in 1940. Much of his native state in the years before had been swept away by the Dust Bowl. Winds had carried the copper-red soil as far east as the Mid-Atlantic to drop it, like gritty rain from a place that had none, onto ships still sailing freely between continents.[1]

Those ships would lose their freedom in the years immediately after, and the coyotes that hunted them without fear were U-boats come out of their lairs in Kiel and later in Lorient. U-boat captains called this the "Happy Time."

The U-boats would someday kill that young fieldworker, if indirectly, as part of an inexorable chain of events that would lead him to Normandy, so far away from the fields that border Arroyo Grande Creek, and to pastures bound by hedges and grazed by fat dairy cows, cows that lowed piteously to be milked in what had become killing zones. One of them, dead in the crossfire, may have provided scant cover for fieldworker, now rifleman, Private Domingo Martinez from the German machine guns that harvested crops of young men.

It is difficult to imagine Normandy in 1944; it is beautiful today, as are its people. A *bonjour* from an American tourist has more traction here than it does in Paris, and the little villages, separated by pastures and farm fields, are lovely, each with its distinctive little parish church. During the Middle Ages, as the skilled writer and Francophile Graham Robb notes, few villagers ever went beyond the sound of their parish church's bells. The world beyond was like the ends of the earth.[2]

It is not the ends of the earth, but the Arroyo Grande Valley is 5,500 miles away from the D-day beaches. Three local men, killed in the campaign to capture and then and break free from Normandy, are buried at the American Cemetery at Colleville-sur-Mer, an almost impossibly serene place above Omaha Beach.

Omaha Beach today. *Author photo.*

Below the cemetery, just offshore, a visitor today can see young men as they should be—exuberant and free—racing tiny sailboats, their sails bright oranges and reds, just beyond the surf line, where on June 6, 1944, young men floated like dead leaves on the water's surface. The invasion of Hitler's Europe nearly failed here. It didn't but only because of an American generation that includes those who still hold the high ground at Colleville-sur-Mer.

Up there, on the immaculate cemetery grounds and not far from a famous American—the ebullient and popular General Theodore Roosevelt Jr., felled by a massive heart attack soon after the invasion—lies a soldier as far removed from the Roosevelts' patrician (if rambunctious) Oyster Bay home as a human being can be. He is Private Domingo Martinez.

Martinez is buried in Plot C, Row 13, Grave 38. He's listed as a farmworker in his 1943 army enlistment papers.[3] Two more soldiers, city boys compared to Martinez, are memorialized at the American Cemetery, both from the county seat, San Luis Obispo, north of Arroyo Grande.

One of them is an artillery officer, Second Lieutenant Claude Newlin, who is buried here. Ironically, Newlin's battalion, attached to the Thirty-fifth Infantry Division, had spent part of its training at Camp San Luis Obispo, just north of his home. Newlin survived some of the costliest fighting of the campaign, near St. Lo, only to die hours before the Thirty-fifth broke out of Normandy to join George Patton's breathtaking race across France to Metz and the German frontier.[4]

For the second San Luis Obispo soldier, an airman, there is a memorial but no grave. On June 22, Second Lieutenant Jack Langston was flying his P-38 in a low-level bombing and strafing attack on Cherbourg with his 367th Fighter Squadron when that city's flak guns demonstrated the folly of ordering low-level attacks. Langston died that day with four other 367th pilots. His body was never recovered.[5]

Far below the speeding fighters and fighter-bombers, Private Martinez was fighting in the suburbs of Cherbourg with the 313th Regiment of the 79th Infantry Division—the "Cross of Lorraine Division," St. Joan's symbol and theirs—which had returned to France a generation after it had seen hard fighting there in 1918.

The division had been sent into action soon after landing on Utah Beach two weeks after D-day. The Seventy-ninth moved west and then turned north to push up the Cherbourg peninsula. The city, at the peninsula's tip, needed to be taken because the Allies faced an enormous logistical problem. They needed a port to help feed, arm and fuel the growing numbers of Allied soldiers in France—the artificial "Mulberry" harbor that allowed the

A P-38 with its D-day markings, much like the plane Jack Langston would've flown. *National Archives.*

offloading of ships off Omaha Beach would be destroyed in a capricious Channel storm. So for the Allied command, Cherbourg was critical.

It was also difficult to take. Its bristling antiaircraft defenses would claim Jack Langston. Massive coastal batteries could keep naval support for the Americans at bay, and the city's *Wehrmacht* defenders, though not elite troops (20 percent of them were non-German conscripts), were securely dug in and had nowhere to go. They were backed into a corner of France and so isolated that the only alternative to fighting was to leap into the sea.

That would have been a blessing for Martinez and the 313th Infantry Regiment, who, on their march north to the suburbs of Cherbourg on the right flank of the 79th Division, learned a bitter lesson in military engineering from the Germans. A network of concrete pillboxes guarded the southern approaches to the city. They contained machine guns pre-sited for interlocking fields of fire for maximum effect on the Americans.

These pillboxes were impervious to frontal attack—57-mm artillery shells bounced off their steel-and-concrete facings—so two battalions of the 313th engaged the enemy while a third looped to the left and came in on the rear of the fortifications, where they were more vulnerable. But as the 313th leap-frogged closer to the city, it discovered that the Germans it thought it had subdued had been hiding deep in underground galleries and had reoccupied some of their fortifications. For a short time, the enemy would cut all of the regiment's contact with divisional headquarters. So the 313th would have to do what both generals and privates hated—fight over the same ground twice.

Once they'd gotten inside Cherbourg, Seventy-ninth Division GIs learned to hate street fighting, as well. Death came instantly from illusory shadows that a fallen soldier's comrades never saw and from gunfire they sometimes never heard. In peacetime, a French city block can be cacophonous with the sounds of café music or cheers inside during the World Cup and the comic honking of little cars or the squeals of children at play. In combat, the same block, seemingly empty, can muffle the report of a sniper's rifle or generate echoes that make soldiers look anxiously in all directions at once.[6]

But Martinez's regiment fought block to block until, on June 26, it reached the water's edge. The 313th then turned its artillery loose on Fort du Roule, which dominated the city. Its commander surrendered later in the day. The men of the 79th, by the time they had finally finished securing the city, were filthy, exhausted and bearded—"like burlesque tramps," as one newspaper reporter said.[7]

After a short rest, the division made the transition from urban combat to a new offensive, a drive through the farmland of the Cotentin Peninsula. This assignment was interrupted briefly on July 4 for a visit from the Brass. Ike and General Omar Bradley, the American ground commander, were with the Seventy-ninth when, on their orders, every American artillery piece in Normandy fired into German lines a simultaneous single-shell barrage to celebrate Independence Day.

Seventy-ninth Division GIs fighting in the streets of Cherbourg. *National Archives.*

The *bocage* country, Normandy, from the air. Each field became a battleground. *National Archives.*

There seemed to be little else to celebrate. By the fourth week after D-day, the Americans were falling short of the objectives set for them by Allied planners and the staff officers working furiously over maps in General Bradley's custom command trailer. The offensive in the Cotentin stalled in great part because the Germans had the advantage of fighting defensively in the *bocage*, the Norman hedgerows, and they began to winnow the Americans down.

The hedgerows enclosed fields that had been plowed or grazed since Agincourt and were a hopscotch of natural fortresses—roots and compacted earth had formed defensible walls. The GIs had to assault them, one by one, to try to root out the defenders. When they broke through a hedge and entered a field, the superb German machine gun, the MG42, hidden in the next hedge beyond or positioned on the Americans' flanks, annihilated entire rifle squads. It fired so rapidly that a burst sounded like canvas ripping. Army films had incorporated the sound to try to desensitize trainees.[8] So the Americans could hear but never see in the tangle of the hedges who was killing them so efficiently. With supreme indifference, the *bocage* quickly transformed GIs into either hardened veterans or into statistics. This is what Private Martinez and the 313th Regiment faced in the attempt to seize the approaches to a key crossroads town, La Haye-du-Puits.

There, the Americans fought first-class combat troops, not garrison soldiers, many of them veterans of the Russian front. As the 313th fought to

In terrain typical of the *bocage* country, artillerymen from Arroyo Grande GI Manuel Gularte's 965th Field Artillery Battalion entertain two guests—little French girls, ribbons in their hair—at lunch. The 965th would later play a key role early in the Battle of the Bulge. *Photo courtesy Beverly Gularte Harben.*

envelop the town, the regiment's combat chronicle is almost monotonous with passages that have the Americans falling back to their jump-off points after repeated failed attacks through fields, then across a creek, where every time they would be driven back by concentrated German artillery fire. The Germans had not only the finest machine gun of the war but also the finest artillery piece, the versatile 88-mm gun.[9]

Other elements of the 79th Division would take La Haye-du-Puits while the 313th Regiment continued its sledgehammer attacks to the south. Martinez died during three furious assaults near a little town called Le Bot on July 12. It was likely an 88-mm shell that killed Martinez. Shrapnel to the head and chest ended his life quickly, but his death wasn't recorded for three days, an indicator of the intensity of the stress the 313th had to endure.[10] The division was victorious, but both the regiment and the division were depleted and their dogfaces, real veterans now, were used up. Signal corps photographers show some 79th soldiers playacting outside a wine shop along a street in La Haye-du-Puits—they sit at a

Seventy-ninth Division GI's move out of La Haye du Puits, 1944. The lead soldier is carrying a mortar tube. One of the soldiers behind has the mortar's baseplate strapped to his back. *National Archives.*

small table amid the rubble, enjoying a fine red wine as if they had dinner reservations and were awaiting the first course. But other photos of other soldiers show men who resemble sleepwalkers: their faces blank and few of them celebratory.

With rest and replacements, the veterans of three weeks' combat soon joined the breakout from Normandy. Two weeks after Martinez's death, the Allies launched Operation Cobra, a coordinated drive to the east. They uncovered Paris and liberated the city in August, standing aside to let Free French units and their prickly commander, General Leclerc, enter first. Leclerc would have been furious to learn that Ernest Hemingway and some of his camp followers had preceded him and were, with great offensive spirit but also with deteriorating unit cohesion, busy liberating the bar at the Ritz Hotel.

It's not hard to wish that Private Martinez had been granted more time—maybe, for this migrant farmworker and Dust Bowl refugee, time enough for a few days' leave to explore Paris. Perhaps he would decide to visit Notre Dame, where it's not hard to see him in your mind's eye. He would enter the great church, remove his garrison cap and cross himself at a

Domingo Martinez's grave at the American Cemetery in Normandy. *Author photo.*

holy water font. Then he would walk up the nave, the silence pressing on his ears, to stand for a moment at the transept crossing, where he would stop to smile with delight as he was bathed in brilliant, colored sunlight. This is the gift of the Rose Window to men and women of good faith.

PART II

SOWING

· ·

Chapter 2

PIONEERS, 1837-1900

The first gunshot heard in the Arroyo Grande Valley came a few weeks before Victoria ascended the English throne. It was probably fired from an 1825 Hawken rifle,[11] and its target might have been either a meal—mule deer creep down from the hills to water at dusk—or an animal that wanted to make the newly arrived rifleman a meal. In 1837, the principal occupants of the Arroyo Grande Valley were grizzly bears. They dominated, unchallenged, what was then *monte*—the Spanish word for a vast wasteland—of marsh, dense with sycamore and cottonwoods.[12] Another newcomer, fur trapper George Nidever, attempting to settle to the east in the Huasna Valley, claimed forty-five bears in 1837 alone, and before he gave up the idea of ranching altogether, estimated that he'd killed close to two hundred.

The man who fired the rifle that April day would not give up and instead would begin to build a home that would headquarter the seventeen-thousand-acre *rancho*, the Santa Manuela, after his wife's namesake. His name was Francis Ziba Branch. At the height of his wealth, the Santa Manuela was the nucleus for a total of seventy-five thousand acres he acquired in southern San Luis Obispo County. Originally from Scipio, New York, he'd become a Mexican citizen and married the daughter, thirteen years his junior, of a comfortable Mexican bureaucrat.

Her name was Manuela Carlón, and she would bear him a small army of eleven children. Some of them, as in any army, would be lost. But this would be a remarkable marriage, and the family would transform the *monte* into a working but multidimensional cattle ranch. The Branches

Francis Ziba Branch. *Courtesy South County Historical Society.*

planted a variety of crops, as well. The Santa Manuela, in its heyday, must have been like a beehive, employing up to thirty people, mostly local Chumash Indians. For the mistress of the Santa Manuela, the little town of Arroyo Grande may have been her twelfth child and her most important, and it was bustling with commerce, progress and boosterism when she died at ninety-four in 1909.[13]

By 1837, her husband had already lived enough lives for three men: a sailor on the Great Lakes; a mountain man and explorer; a businessman in Santa Barbara, where he'd met Manuela; and now a rancher. He was one of the Anglo-American *rancheros* who dominated the early recorded history of California, and in a frontier like the southern part of San Luis Obispo County, it was not a long history, preceded only by mission fathers who planted fruit orchards and vineyards in the Corralitos Canyon of the Upper Arroyo Grande Valley and vegetable gardens along the creek.

Mexican independence and the secularization of the mission properties would lead to a new wave of settlers.

Among them were Branch, a New Yorker; William Dana, a Bostonian; and John Price, an Englishman, who would marry Manuela Carlón Branch's sister. These men owned tens of thousands of acres and bred cattle—for beef, hides and tallow—and they had to fight to keep them; both grizzlies, wiped out within a generation, and Tulare Indians, who sometimes made raids from the San Joaquin Valley, were problematic for these tough and determined men. A fourth, Isaac Sparks, who sold John Price the eight-thousand-acre Rancho Pismo, took up where George Nidever left off. He settled the wildest backcountry of all, beyond the Arroyo Grande Valley, and established the Huasna Ranch. Sparks would lose an eye in an encounter with one grizzly but, of the four, is the only man whose descendants still run cattle on a working ranch, the Porter Ranch, today.[14]

It was a time when men were as savage, if not more so, than the rapidly dwindling grizzly bears. In the County Historical Museum in San Luis Obispo, nineteenth-century coroner's reports were once kept in what resembled an old-time library card catalogue, and every little drawer revealed an adventure when it was opened. On delicate blue parchment, in the elegant cursive of Victorian America, a researcher can find reports on cowboys' bodies found on the wild Cuesta Grade north of San Luis Obispo. One reads, with great precision and economy, "Cause of death: Pistol ball through heart."

When a merciless gang of ship jumpers and goldfield refugees murdered an innkeeper and ten servants and children, including an unborn baby, at Mission San Miguel in the north county in 1848, it was another former mountain man like Branch who found the bodies. "Medicine Jim" Beckwourth rode sixty-two miles south to William Dana's Rancho Nipomo to deliver the news; later, Branch and John Price—an *alcalde*, or justice of the peace—who had themselves been visiting the gold fields, inspected the grisly murder scene, and Price turned out a posse of outraged citizens to pursue the killers.

It was a second posse of Santa Barbarans who finally caught up to the men more than ninety miles south of the Arroyo Grande Valley near what is now the little town of Summerland. They were not particularly willing to surrender. There was a running gun battle before they were captured. One was shot; another was drowned; and the remaining three were tried, convicted and then executed by a firing squad commanded by a future Civil War general, then Lieutenant Edward O.C. Ord.[15]

This illustration accompanied a biography of James Beckwourth written in 1855, seven years after he'd discovered the murdered Reed family at Mission San Miguel. Beckwourth (1798–1866), an African American born in Virginia, would become a celebrity in his own lifetime for his exploits as a mountain man and explorer.

When outlaws like Jack Powers and Pio Linares terrorized the area in the 1850s, citizens formed the inevitable Vigilance Committee, and as was the case on the frontier, a spate of hangings—one made the front page of the *New York Times* in 1853[16]—seemed to end the outlaw era. A more decisive force for change came with a new wave of immigrants who built schools, courthouses,

The Branch family graveyard. *Author photo.*

shops and churches throughout San Luis Obispo County and, eventually, on land the public-spirited Branch donated, constructed those same service buildings in what would become the town of Arroyo Grande.

Yet it was an incomplete civilization. A tragedy central to Branch's life can still be seen in the family's little burying ground. Three small tombstones that flank Branch's tell the most poignant story. Branch's adobe ranch house was, as was customary among the *rancheros*, a stopping place for travelers. One of them brought smallpox there in 1862. Branch, away on business in San Francisco, was summoned home. By the time he arrived, five-year-old Luisa and sixteen-year-old Josefa were already dead; fourteen-year-old Manuela would die shortly after.

Branch now had to face a second tragedy. The 1860s marked a turning point for the *rancheros* and the beginning of the end of their dominance of the area. They had eradicated grizzlies and killers, but they had no weapons to use against the drought that came then and returns in cycles. Twenty-first-century Californians are as helpless as was Branch and watch anxiously in dry years when, in the fall, the yellow and brittle hills of Central and Southern California catch fire and send pillars of smoke far into the skies.

When the cattle died, so did Branch's fortune. The 1862–63 drought cost him $400,000—roughly $8 million today—at the same time that he had lost his daughters. What would have broken another man's spirit seemed only to energize Branch. It was during the 1860s that he laid down the plan for Arroyo Grande's town streets. He had always been a sophisticated businessman and had generated income in a variety of ways—including using the Arroyo Grande Creek to turn a millstone that ground the valley's grain into flour—and began to shift to dairy farming. He was fighting his way back when he died. He was buried, in 1874, next to his little girls.

The taming of the Arroyo Grande Valley begun by Branch should have accelerated with the 1881 arrival of the railroad, the narrow-gauge Pacific Coast Railroad (PCRR). The railroad did, to a large extent, continue to civilize the valley, tying it to the Pacific Ocean. The track ran to the end of a commercial wharf at Port Harford, forty miles south to Los Olivos; to markets for Arroyo Grande produce in the county seat, San Luis Obispo, sixteen miles to the north; and then, via the Union Pacific, to more distant places.[17]

The railroad's efficacy as a tool of civilization was weakened in 1886, when the citizens of Arroyo Grande hanged a fifteen-year-old boy from the PCRR bridge that forded the Arroyo Grande Creek in the heart of town. The lynch mob strung up the boy's father, too, and the bodies were left dangling for hours. Little boys slipped away from school and stood under the corpses to gawk at them, from the soles of their feet to their stricken, clay-colored faces.

It was a living face that one witness never forgot. Fred Jones, the grandson of Francis Branch, in very old age, talked to my elder brother's class at our little school in the late 1950s. The victims of the vigilantes were Peter Hemmi and his son, Julius, or P.J. Fred Jones was fourteen when this happened, and said his father never forgave himself for bringing him along to see another teenager die the way this one did.

Jones remembered that Mrs. Hemmi was waiting while her husband, son and a nephew were being held in what passed for a town jail when the vigilantes, some wearing masks, burst in. The look on her face revealed, Jones said, that she knew exactly what was about to happen, and that image haunted him for the rest of his life.

They wanted to lynch Peter's nephew, but Peter insisted that he was not involved in the crime they wanted to avenge. The mob let the nephew go, and he ran for his life with a noose still around his neck and a length of thick rope trailing after.[18]

However, Peter could not save his son. P.J. was, longtime local historian Madge Ditmas once wrote, a boy of "cruel disposition,"[19] and he had ended a long-running boundary dispute over property near the source of Arroyo Grande Creek with a rifle. In a confrontation between the Hemmis and their neighbor, Eugene Walker, P.J. began shooting. Walker died in his garden, amid his vegetables. P.J. then shot Walker's dog and, finally, shot Mrs. Walker twice. She lived, but just hours later, no amount of pleading could save the terrified boy. This was justice.

There was not the slightest chance that the two would be allowed burial on sanctified ground amid their neighbors. So seventy-one-year-old Manuela Branch had their bodies brought to her family's graveyard, and the two were buried twenty feet away from her husband, whose reputation was indestructible. By the early 1960s, the little burial ground had reverted to pasture, and generations of cattle with itches to scratch had knocked down, one by one, the elegant Victorian obelisks and tablets that had marked the graves of the pioneer family. But at some point, someone had built a heavy-gauge steel pipe fence around the graves of Julius and P.J., so their

This tombstone over the Hemmis' grave in the Branch family graveyard was part of an Eagle Scout project in the early 1970s; the original markers were destroyed. *Author photo.*

tombstones stood upright and unrepentant. Somehow, later that decade, they were destroyed.

The Hemmi lynching was an anomaly in the history of Arroyo Grande. The time between the drought years and the First World War was marked by progress and by an influx of farmers who succeeded *rancheros* like Branch, Price and Dana. Branch's son Fred continued to sell small pieces of the Santa Manuela Ranch to farmers arriving in his valley.[20]

So a new generation settled Arroyo Grande. There were easterners like Branch himself, including Charles Pitkin of Connecticut, who built an elegant mansion for his family that today is a bed-and-breakfast and still surrounded by farm fields; some settlers came from England—which accounts for the road cheerily named "Tally Ho" by the immigrant Vachells, occasional polo players, and Englishman L.D. Waller, who arrived in 1905 and began cultivating seed flowers.

Branch's descendants, the offspring of the Santa Manuela ranchero, would take their places among this new generation settling the valley. His daughter Anna had married Virginian David F. Newsom in 1863, and the two farmed 1,200 acres of what was now called "the Branch Tract." Newsom, like his father-in-law, who had started a school on the Santa Manuela Ranch, was intensely interested in education. He championed school construction and served on school district boards.[21] Branch's sons—including Ramón, whose adobe remains where he worked 4,000 acres—continued to farm. The old home is today a tasting room for the vineyards belonging to another prominent farm family, the Talleys.[22]

The town site that Anna and Ramón's father had donated, the one whose main street bears his name, continued to grow into the new century and incorporated in 1911. A smithy, retail businesses—E.C. Loomis's feed store and F.E. Bennett's Grocery among them—a town newspaper and, at the foot of Crown Hill on the eastern end of town, the regular passage of the busy little narrow-gauge locomotive were all indicators that times were changing and rapidly.

There were still episodes of frontier violence. In February 1904, town marshal Henry Lewelling entered the Capitol Saloon to disarm a man who'd been firing his revolver in the air along Branch Street. The gunman shot the peace officer in the chest; Lewelling collapsed in the saloon doorway and died thirty agonizing hours later in the Ryan Hotel.[23]

But saloons like the Capitol faced competition from churches, and sometimes, their paths crossed. Historian Jean Hubbard recorded the history of a prominent early church, First United Methodist, including the time that

Clara Edwards, the future Clara Paulding, just before her first
assignment as a teacher/governess in Hawaii, 1881. *Courtesy South County
Historical Society.*

Pastor Osborn's sermon was interrupted by a befuddled drunk who wandered
into the church. Osborn stopped; grabbed the trespasser by the collar;
dragged him outside; and, after the noise of "a brief scuffle," nonchalantly
reentered and finished that Sunday's lesson.[24]

St. Barnabas Episcopal Church's most faithful parishioner might have
been Miss Ruth Paulding, a longtime teacher at the high school and a link to
the earliest days of the town. She was born in 1892 and grew up in a large
home on Crown Hill that was framed, when I was growing up, by venerable
shade trees, vegetable gardens and immense sunflowers. Ruth's commute
was brief. She had to walk only across the street to reach the high school.

Her hero and role model was her mother, Clara, about whom she wrote a small biography, *The Gallant Lady*.

Clara was a teacher, too, partly out of necessity. Her husband, Ruth's father, was town physician Dr. Ed Paulding, but the little family needed Clara's income, modest as it was, to help pay for the home they'd bought on Crown Hill. Both mother and daughter loved teaching and loved learning. In fact, long after her retirement, Clara returned to college with Ruth during World War II, when a revived economy allowed the high school to promise Ruth an extra $100 a year if she took additional coursework. The pair decided to take summer courses at Clara's alma mater, Mills College. Ruth took classes for the extra money; Clara, over eighty years old, took hers for pleasure, including a course in the "History of the United States to 1865" because, she said, she remembered the rest.

One of Clara's assignments during more than thirty years in the classroom was Branch Elementary, tucked into a corner of the upper valley, about five hundred yards from where the *ranchero*'s adobe once stood. There is an 1898 photo of her in front of the school; behind Clara and the new machine that did so much to liberate Victorian women—the bicycle—are the same steps I would climb on my first day of formal education sixty years later. Like most teachers of the time, she was fearless and ran a tight ship, but she had the greatest gift a good teacher can possibly have: she loved children, and they knew it.[25]

A worker turns over a field on Waller Seed Company land at about the time of the First World War. Horses were essential to Arroyo Grande Valley agriculture for years. *Courtesy Richard Waller.*

By 1900, Arroyo Grande's population was approaching one thousand. Beyond the town—to the east in the upper valley and to the west, bounded by the sand dunes at the edge of the Pacific, in the lower valley—there were patchworks of farm fields plowed by ambitious men who drove draft horses, their necks arched in effort as they turned some of the richest soil in the world. They might have been sowing pumpkins or carrots, onions or beans or one of the most important products in the many cycles of agriculture the valley has seen: flowers, cultivated for their seeds.[26]

What must have delighted Clara Paulding on her two-mile bicycle commute to her students every morning was the sight of brilliant fields of flowers and the delicate fragrance of sweet peas. By the early part of the new century, some of the workers in those fields, their wide-brimmed straw hats looking like mushroom caps as they bent to their work, would figure prominently in the American history that Clara loved. They were the first immigrants to arrive from Japan, most of them from the southern island, Kyushu, but a few of them from Honshu, farther north, in Hiroshima prefecture.

CHAPTER 3

THE IMMIGRANTS, 1900-1941

Like Branch himself, the heritage of mid-nineteenth-century Arroyo Grande Valley was a distinct Mexican/Yankee hybrid. In the twentieth century, immigration would introduce new cultural traditions. At the IDES (*Irmandade do Divino Espirito Santa*) Hall on the edge of town, locals still celebrate Portuguese *festas*, where barbecue and thick, rich *sopa*, or stew, commemorates the kind of diet that can keep a man hard at work—at whaling or farming, for example—for hours at a time and still sustain his strength. Fourth-generation Japanese girls, lovely and graceful, still perform the Coal Miners' Dance at Obon, a festival that comes every fall, sponsored by the Buddhist Church, which features *bonsai* for quieter visitors and taiko drumming for livelier tastes. The village of Arroyo Grande commemorates its agricultural heritage every year at the Harvest Festival, and there is only one pleasure greater than eating a Filipino *lumpia*, or egg roll, and that is to see the reaction of the members of the Filipino Women's Club booth after you've take your first bite and closed your eyes in delight.

So the fifty years after 1874, the year of Branch's death, were marked by these three successive waves of immigrants who have added a cultural richness and a powerful sense of commitment to family, community service and serving their adopted nation. In return, sometimes both community and nation seemed hell-bent on driving the newcomers out.

For a people who had traveled so far, the Portuguese who farmed the valley seemed most comfortable when they took the time to come to a complete stop. In a phenomenon any American can see in eastern Colorado, the

Texas panhandle or southern Missouri—one I saw growing up in the upper valley—two farmers, like Manuel and Johnny Silva, who just had breakfast together two hours before, would stop in the middle of a rural road, pickup cab to pickup cab, to talk while sprinklers described vast arcs in the fields alongside them. It was a mystery what they would have to talk about so soon after breakfast, but if a motorist had come up behind one of the trucks, the men inside would instantly pull off to the side to let him by. Two hundred yards later, if the motorist had looked in his rearview mirror, the trucks would be together again, and the conversation would have resumed. Moments like those, seventy years after their ancestors had come to America, demonstrated that the secret to the success of Portuguese immigrants in the Arroyo Grande Valley was their devotion to one another.

Not everyone had a benevolent view of the Portuguese. When a massive earthquake and tsunami destroyed Lisbon in 1755, Italian Jesuit Gabriel Malagrida argued that the Portuguese had invited disaster for their multitude of sins, which he catalogued and explicated in a famous essay. In so doing, Malagrida generated aftershocks of his own in a flurry of essays written by Enlightenment *philosophes* and less-than-precise scientists that challenged his explanation for the disaster. This culminated with the upstart Rousseau publicly and bitingly denouncing the venerable Voltaire for his despair over the disaster and its meaning. Meanwhile, John Wesley, the founder of Methodism, had the temerity to argue in a sermon that God loved human beings, including Lisboans, and did not cause earthquakes to punish sinners.[27]

But it was violent seismic activity like that in Lisbon that helped spur a great immigration of the people of the Azores to the United States. A series of earthquakes and volcanic eruptions, along with economic stagnation and political unrest, led nineteenth-century Azoreans to leave for Brazil or the United States. Today, their American descendants outnumber the remaining Azoreans four to one.[28] They would settle continental America from Boston to San Luis Obispo County and would take up a familiar trade, whaling, in Hawaii and along the California coast. Portuguese immigrants to San Luis Obispo launched boats from San Simeon, where they harvested primarily gray whales and, occasionally, a humpback. But by the 1870s, harvests were dwindling, and John D. Rockefeller was instead harvesting lesser oil companies to build Standard Oil. Kerosene and, later, Edison's incandescent light bulb forced the seafaring Azoreans to look inland.[29]

In Arroyo Grande, Portuguese immigrants turned to dairy farming and the cultivation of vegetables. The immigrants were both skilled farmers and devout Catholics, so their *festas*—including the Festival of the Holy Spirit,

IDES Parade, Branch Street, about 1913. *Courtesy South County Historical Society.*

which commemorates the generosity and miracles attributed to thirteenth-century queen Isabel of Portugal—became a regular feature of the growing town's life. Parades down Branch Street, barbecues and dances organized by the religious fraternity IDES (*Irmandade do Divino Espirito Santa*) made the Portuguese a highly visible minority and might have hastened what seems like a relatively brief period of assimilation into the community.[30]

The *festa* is still an annual event centered at the IDES Hall just outside town, and Portuguese Americans from the San Joaquin Valley descend on nearby Pismo Beach in the late summer for the St. Anthony Festival, a tradition that began in the mid-1950s. In Arroyo Grande, while parish priests were Irish, it was the Portuguese who would be the backbone of St. Patrick's Catholic Church, which stood, in the kind of harmony John Wesley might have liked, within a few feet of the Methodist church that flanked it to the east.

Festa celebrants before the war years would have included the Brown family. Antonio and his wife, Anna, were both born in the Azores, became citizens in 1906, presumably had their names Anglicized and produced two sons widely spread apart in age. Lionel was born in 1904 and his younger brother, Louis, in 1924, when both parents were in their early forties. Louis must have seemed like another one of Queen Isabel's miracles.[31]

The Browns were farmers and settled just outside Arroyo Grande in Corbett Canyon, narrow and dense with oaks but with pockets of good soil that the immigrants began to cultivate. Today, the canyon is noted for its horse ranches, where tourists and locals alike pull their cars to the shoulder of the road to watch an Arab filly suddenly bolt from her mother's side to gallop, for the sheer joy of it, on long legs that she's just begun to master. Eventually, like human toddlers, she will collapse and go to sleep.

The Browns must have known a much larger family with difficult circumstances. Their neighbors, José and Clara Gularte, came from the Azores early in the century and married in San Luis Obispo in 1906. In the 1920s, José, or Joseph, began to cultivate strawberries, helping to pioneer what would become an important area crop. The berries were harvested by a platoon of his daughters, and their father made sales rounds to the Portuguese groceries in San Luis Obispo. Joseph died suddenly in 1934, and Clara became the head of a family of ten children: four boys and six girls. Clara's burden would have been lightened by her elder sons, who took over the family's farm; the 1940 census shows that the girls were beginning to marry and establish households of their own.[32] A younger son, Frank, was working for one of the most important businesses in the valley, E.C. Loomis and Son, vegetable brokers who kept a farm supply and feed store at the base of Crown Hill in Arroyo Grande.

The feed store—whose building still stands today—was central to the life of the town. It was stocked with everything from leather harnesses, stiff and shiny, to great fortresses of baled hay and from big gunny sacks of sweet-smelling mash—it would have taken a strong man to lift them—to racks of incubators full of fuzzy chicks, all of them habitual speechmakers.

This is where the farmers of the upper and lower valleys, uniformed in faded denim overalls and battered felt hats, would gather for gossip as well as business. They were incurable talkers, like E.C.'s chicks. Since the Loomises were known for their hospitality—which means there's a good chance that Frank, by extension, was outgoing and popular—so those farmers might have been in no great hurry to get back to work. The circle of men who traded news and jokes included the Azoreans, who had found a permanent place in the life of the valley. The place of the next wave of immigrants, the Japanese, would be more precarious despite the warmth the Loomis family extended to them.

They began to arrive on the West Coast in the 1890s. In Arroyo Grande, most of them were from the southernmost of the home islands, Kyushu, and many from Kagoshima prefecture. Other families, like Ben Dohi's and

Joseph Gularte and his daughters—including Barbara, the youngest (foreground)—picking strawberries in the 1920s. *Photo courtesy Annie Gularte Silva.*

The E.C. Loomis Building, at the foot of Crown Hill, today. *Author photo.*

Mits Fukuhara's, came from Hiroshima prefecture on Honshu, "on the other side of the hill," from the devastated city, Dohi said in a 2008 interview. After the war, when he served as an army interpreter during the Occupation, Dohi was stationed in Kagoshima and made a point to visit the villages where his boyhood friends had their ancestral roots. The United States beckoned to the parents of Dohi's friends at the turn of the century, when their own nation was eager to export them—interestingly, because of their fidelity.

The arrival of significant numbers of Japanese workers in Arroyo Grande had its origins in the collapse of the longtime shogunate, or military dictatorship, begun by Tokugawa Ieyasu in the seventeenth century. In 1867, Japanese leadership passed to the dynamic young Mutsuhito, the Meiji emperor. The Meiji government was determined to make Japan, after centuries of isolation, a part of the world community and an industrial superpower, as well. To finance its modernization programs—they would include building a modern military shaped by advisors from the German army and British navy—the government instituted a new land tax that generated income but also hardship: 370,000 farmers lost their land between 1880 and 1900 because of tax defaults.

The potential for social unrest was immense, but the timing was opportune. In 1882, the United States, amid one of the periodic cycles of xenophobia that have marked our history, had passed the Chinese Exclusion Act. Ironically, the saviors of the Meiji Empire, in one small way, were foreign labor contractors from Hawaii and the mainland United States, eager for the kind of men who had the kind of work ethic that the Chinese had demonstrated. The emperor's government embraced the Americans and pointed them immediately to Kyushu.

The government did so because Kyushu historically had been the region most resistant to the Tokugawa shoguns, and by extension, the new emperor trusted his subjects there the most. And by recruiting thousands of them to work crops like Hawaiian sugar cane, the foreign labor contractors were defusing a social crisis for the landowners and prefects who were the most helpful in consolidating unification of Meiji Japan.

Secondly, according to historian Sucheng Chan, a scholar of East Asian immigration to America, Mutsuhito trusted the self-discipline and the industry of the sons raised in Kagoshima prefecture. They would send money home, which would further ease social tension, an assumption that would prove to be accurate. The government of the Meiji period, meanwhile, was astute enough to keep potential seditionists from the other islands close at hand. [33] This shows a political acuity the Romanov family lacked when they deported Lenin, who returned with a vengeance to plant the seeds for the Bolshevik Revolution that would lead to the deaths of the royal family one year later.

While some Japanese immigrants to Hawaii and mainland America, like many young Italian men, intended their stays to be temporary in order to send money home to families hard-pressed by taxes, others would opt to settle here, and they had to have been uniquely determined men because the government threw a bewildering number of legal roadblocks in their way. Since these immigrants were not white, they were not eligible for citizenship, as affirmed in an 1894 Supreme Court ruling. In October 1906, the San Francisco Board of Education, alarmed by the increasing numbers of Japanese, voted to segregate Asian students in the schools of the city, a measure that outraged the Japanese government. In 1908, however, that government and the United States agreed to the "Gentleman's Agreement," which brought most Japanese immigration to a halt. Not yet satisfied, the California legislature in Sacramento passed not one but two Alien Land

Laws, in 1913 and 1920, which forbade "aliens ineligible for citizenship"—which meant all immigrant Japanese—from owning land and, later, from even leasing it.[34]

But Arroyo Grande's Ella Honeycutt, a longtime conservationist and a gifted agricultural historian, notes that by 1913, when California legislators passed the first Alien Land Law, it was too late. Many local immigrant families had already acquired farms. They tended to concentrate in the lower Arroyo Grande Valley, where they grew vegetables, especially bush and pole peas, and when the latter were hit by disease in the mid-1920s, they began to grow newer crops like celery, lettuce and Chinese cabbage.[35] The newcomers hunted for legal loopholes and found them. They formed corporations and bought land through them or through friendly white intermediaries, or they bought land in the names of their American-born children, whose citizenship would be inviolable until Executive Order 9066 proved otherwise. The birth of that new generation of Japanese Americans—the Nisei—was proof incarnate that the people from Kyushu intended to stay in the valley and make it their home. This trend was made possible by a single premeditated

Kimi Kobara came to America as a picture bride, as did these Japanese women, arriving at Angel Island, San Francisco, about 1920. *National Archives.*

and humane opening in the anti-Japanese laws. They allowed those men already in American to settle here with their wives, to send home for them or to send, as if they came from the Sears catalogue, for "picture brides."

This is how Shigechika Kobara, one of the early immigrants to the valley, and his wife, Kimi, began their lives together. Their fathers were neighbors in Kagoshima, and after a short negotiation and a longer courtship, by letter, the match was made. Shigechika took a train north and was waiting on a Seattle dock, looking for his bride among the passengers on her ship as it began to berth. She was looking back. "I remembered his brother, a naval officer," Kimi recalled, "and I found a man who resembled him. I thought that this was the man I was about to marry. From the deck, I fixed my eyes on him, even though I had never met him. That is why it is called a 'picture bride.'"[36]

Life in Arroyo Grande dismayed the middle-class, somewhat sheltered Mrs. Kobara. While her husband got up every morning at 4:00 a.m. to groom and harness the draft horses for his boss, Mr. Tomooka, Kimi sat alone in the bed and wondered what she'd gotten into. She wondered every morning; she cried every night.

The marriage would last six decades.

So it was married couples who were among the earliest Japanese to settle in Arroyo Grande. The Saruwatari family might have been the first and are still here. Both Kinzo and his wife, Morio, arrived in America in 1901. In February 1918, Juzo Ikeda and his wife, Sei, landed in Seattle aboard the *Kotari Maru* (although Juzo had originally come to California in 1906, when his ship docked in Oakland because San Francisco was burning). Yeiju Hayashi came to Seattle on Christmas Eve 1919 on the *Kashima Maru*; his wife, Toyo, followed, landing in San Francisco on the *Siberia Maru* the following June. Some families arrived in Arroyo Grande after having worked and lived in Hawaii. Shiuchi Kawaoka came to Arroyo Grande in 1912 but not as an "alien." He had been born in Hawaii in 1896, the year American sugar planters, led by Sanford Dole, ended Hawaiian sovereignty by deposing Queen Liliuokalani, so Shiuchi was an American.[37]

But the most important force for Americanization may have been baseball, and in Arroyo Grande, the primary agent of assimilation would be E.C. Loomis's son, Vard, a former pitcher for Stanford and now part of the family's farm supply business. Vard, a big, handsome and affable man, liked to talk baseball with his Japanese customers during his sales calls to their lettuce fields, and the Loomises hosted a barbecue every year for the Japanese. Yeiju Hayashi would make huge tubs of seafood-and-lettuce salads, and the eating and cigars would be followed by baseball. It was Juzo Ikeda who asked Vard if he would be interested in managing a Japanese American baseball team. Vard was. The Arroyo Grande Growers, shepherded by Vard and his wife, Gladys, went barnstorming, playing other Japanese teams up and down the coast and in the San Joaquin Valley. Juzo's sons played for Vard, as they would for the high school and the local state college, Cal Poly, in San Luis Obispo. One of them—Kazuo, or Kaz—would be the catcher, and his friendship with Vard would be tested in the months after the attack on Pearl Harbor.[38]

With the arrival of the twentieth century, another immigrant group, Filipinos, became Americans, after a fashion. They lived in a kind of limbo: they had U.S. passports, but they encountered intense racism when they, like the young men from Kagoshima, came to America to work. The process of assimilation, in fact, had begun at gunpoint in the same decade of imperial adventure that had ended Liliuokalani's reign in Hawaii. Neither she nor the Filipino people—led by a cultivated, dedicated and tragic national hero, Emilio Aguinaldo—had any intention of becoming Americans.

In 1898, Filipino patriots allied themselves with the United States in the war that began and ended that year against Spain. The islands' name had been taken from one prominent in the Hapsburg family. It was Philip

The P.I. Market, Pismo Beach, which was both a grocery and a community center for local Filipino immigrants. *Courtesy the Cal Poly Special Collections and Archives, Lucille Lor Collection.*

II who'd been humiliated by an earlier English-speaking power in the spectacular defeat of his armada. His family, marked by the deformity called the Hapsburg jaw, was strong-chinned and in all other things weak, and Spain, from the seventeenth century onward, would begin a long but steady decline as a European power. So the Filipinos, ruled as the Americans had been by a distant monarchy, hoped to find in the United States a sponsor like the one we had found in France during our war for independence.

And so we agreed to play the role. While Aguinaldo led the Filipino resistance to Spanish troops on land, George Dewey, dispatched ahead of the declaration of war by the assistant secretary of the navy, Theodore Roosevelt, steamed his fleet into Manila Bay and utterly destroyed the entire Spanish Asiatic Fleet at the cost of one American sailor, who died of heat stroke. And there, a jubilant Aguinaldo and his people must have thought it over. Spain, finally at its imperial sunset, signed a Treaty of Paris and washed their hands of the Philippines.

Theodore Roosevelt, who became the leader of the Wyoming cowboys and Harvard polo players who called themselves the Rough Riders, had no more respect for his own president than Elizabeth I had for Philip. In the lead up to the Spanish-American War, so successfully manufactured in the

The end of the Philippine Insurrection. Filipino soldiers stack arms during their surrender, 1902. *National Archives.*

yellow journalism of newspaper rivals Hearst and Pulitzer, TR had hissed that McKinley was timid, with "all the backbone of a chocolate éclair." Now, McKinley had not only led his country into a war but had also won it, and among the things he had won were twenty million Filipinos. He decided we would keep them. It was our duty, he intoned solemnly, to "uplift and civilize and Christianize them,"[39] oblivious to the fact that 80 percent of the "upliftees" were devout Catholics, but McKinley's sentiment was typical of late Victorian America, which saw itself as thoroughly Protestant and as certain in all things it did as John Calvin had been.

Aguinaldo declined McKinley's offer of civilization, which led to a three-year war marked by savagery on the part of the "civilizers." American brigadier general Jacob Smith, for example, ordered a marine subordinate to kill every Filipino over ten in the pacification of Samar, in retribution for an insurgent attack that had killed fifty-one American soldiers. The marine officer quoted Smith later, at the general's court-martial: "I want no prisoners. I want you to kill and burn, and the more you kill and burn, the more it will please me."[40] It was in the Philippines where American soldiers first used the interrogation technique that would become known as waterboarding, and it was here where a private in a Washington volunteer regiment wrote this in a letter home:

A burying detail from our regiment buried forty-nine nigger enlisted men and two nigger officers, and when we stopped chasing them the night before, we could see 'em carrying a great many with them. We are supposed to have killed about three hundred. Take my advice, and don't enlist in the regulars, for you are good for three years. I am not sorry I enlisted, but you see we have had some excitement and we only have about fourteen months' time to serve, if they keep us our full time, which is not likely. We will, no doubt, start home as soon as we get these niggers rounded up.[41]

American intellectuals reacted with revulsion to the reports of atrocities on the part of their countrymen. "God damn the United States," William James said, "and her vile conduct in the Philippine Isles." Samuel Clemens was less blunt but perhaps more effective in his devastating essay, "To the Brother Sitting in Darkness," and the war that would become known as the Philippine Insurrection divided American combatants just as it divided public opinion at home. In another soldier's letter home, a Nebraskan wrote that "some think the insurgents are disheartened, but I think they will make a desperate struggle for what they consider their rights. I do not approve of the course our government is pursuing with these people. If all men are created equal, they have some rights which ought to be respected."[42]

Fighting for those rights wore Aguinaldo and his countrymen down. A starving resistance leader came out of the wilderness and surrendered in 1902—at least a quarter million of his people, overwhelmingly civilians, had died with only the faintest justice to balance the scales. McKinley, a gallant man who draped a handkerchief over his wife's head during her epileptic seizures, was visiting Buffalo the previous year and had been so taken with a pretty little girl that he instinctively removed his lucky red carnation, gave it to her and then walked into an exhibition hall, where he was immediately shot. That pistol shot would bring Roosevelt into the Oval Office, but it was McKinley's decision to keep his imperial prize that would bring the first Filipinos—someday, Americans—to the Arroyo Grande Valley.

They were overwhelmingly young men—called the Manong ("Older Brother") Generation. As is the case with so many immigrants, they intended to stay here only temporarily to earn enough to go home and start a family or to help improve the fortunes of a birth family, but their labor in the fields and in restaurant kitchens paid little. Soon the young men became trapped in a twilight world. They were an ocean away from home and struggling to survive in a hostile place: "Filipinos," notes ethnic studies professor Grace Yeh of Cal Poly–San Luis Obispo, "were confronted with legal, economic, and social limitations that created bachelor societies, or tigertowns. They were prevented from becoming citizens or from marrying, had little opportunity outside of wage labor, and were looked upon as a social menace."[43]

They weren't looked at that way by a group of boys on Allen Street in Arroyo Grande. John Robison and his friends attended a church school, and two young men delighted in joining their ball games at recess. Afrin Fernando and Benny Goodwell were Filipino immigrants who made a kind of surrogate family there out of the neighborhood kids. Their backyard, with an immaculate garden and a fishpond, was sometimes overrun by a platoon of ten-year-olds in overalls.[44]

To an outsider, on the eve of war, Arroyo Grande must have seemed idyllic. Nowhere is this more apparent than in the old home movies, especially the movie of the Harvest Festival parade in 1937, kept by the historians of the Bennett and Loomis families, longtime residents and Branch Street merchants. This event was the first in what is still a popular and appropriate observance for a farming town. The parade had clutches of little hoboes, maybe reflective of the Depression reality in a town with its own little railroad, as well as the high school band with two majorettes, high-wheeled bicycles, a shiny fire engine, farm wagons and elegant buggies—the latter, still well-maintained but destined soon to become flower planters.

Life was less idyllic for those who worked the crops that drove the local economy. Living conditions for Filipino fieldworkers were abysmal: they slept in thinly partitioned cubicles, prepared meals in kitchens no bigger than old-fashioned telephone booths and appalled health inspectors with the sanitary conditions in their labor camps. On New Year's Day 1937, they went out on a strike directed against Japanese American pea growers, and it grew ugly, including fights between Filipino fieldworkers and more recent arrivals from Japan or Hawaii. It took NLRB intervention and an agreement on growers' part to raise wages from thirty to thirty-five cents per hamper, ending the strike at the end of the month.

The contradiction, of course, is that it had not been that long since the Japanese growers had themselves been laborers and been seen, as the Filipinos were seen during the Great Depression, as an unwelcome people who depressed wages. (Other new arrivals, Dust Bowl refugees, were seen similarly; Dorothea's iconic "Migrant Mother" photograph had been taken just south of Arroyo Grande, in a camp alongside Nipomo pea fields.) Douglas Jentzen described that earlier anti-Japanese sentiment, common in 1908, in a master's thesis in history at Cal Poly–San Luis Obispo:

> *"The town here is strongly opposed to Orientals and has always been noted for so being in the past,"* reported the [San Luis Obispo] Tribune. *"By working and living cheaper they have gradually driven out the white working population and where ever they have succeeded in doing so they have started stores where the Japs do all their trading."* The article continued complaining about how Japanese stores also serve as local employment agencies to help other Japanese immigrants find work on land or crops. It threatened, *"This is not a pretty picture to contemplate, but it is within the bounds of possibility in the Arroyo Grande Valley if the Japs are permitted to gain a foothold here."*[45]

But by the time of the pea strike, Japanese immigrants in southern San Luis Obispo and northern Santa Barbara Counties were remarkably successful growers and were gradually becoming more integrated into the community, as were their children, the Nisei, who, by 1941, were making a mark on the playing fields and in the classrooms of Arroyo Grande schools. It would take the attack on Pearl Harbor to reveal the depth of the envy that their success had generated in some of their neighbors.

PART III

TERRIBLE HARVEST

· ·

CHAPTER 4

THE FIRST CASUALTIES

A Japanese photographer far above Battleship Row on December 7, 1941, captured an image that looks like a cotton boll, far below, on the water's surface. It is, in fact, the concussion of a 1,760-pound bomb that extinguished the life of twenty-two-year-old Musician Third Class Jack Leo Scruggs. The sailor-trombonist and his bandmates were interrupted during the colors ceremony on the fantail of the battleship *Arizona*. The national anthem was silenced by the bomb's explosion, and Scruggs's parents had the small comfort of bringing him home. Jack's body was recovered from the oily water alongside the great ship, its back broken moments later by another bomb explosion in a forward powder magazine.[46]

Scruggs grew up in Arroyo Grande. Another sailor, Seaman First Class Wayne Morgan, also grew up here and remains part of the *Arizona* crew—among those whose bodies were never recovered. Although Scruggs spent only part of his childhood in Arroyo Grande, the odds against having two men from the same little hometown die onboard must be astronomical—except when compared, of course, to those of twenty-three sets of brothers being killed on the ship that day.

We know little about Morgan, even though his father was a fairly prominent man, as the owner of the first Ford agency in town. Morgan would get a headline in the *Arroyo Grande Herald-Recorder* on December 26,[47] but the damage and the humiliation inflicted on the Pacific fleet were still so raw that the story did not connect him with the great ship, the ship that soon would be immortalized because of the unspeakably violent way it was sunk.

A Japanese photograph shows two bombs—a near-miss and a hit—on the stern of the USS *Arizona*, at far left, just inboard of the repair ship *Vestal*. This is the moment of Jack Scruggs's death. *National Archives*.

We know a lot about Jack Scruggs because of his love for music.

His father lost a Hanford fruit ranch in the depression that wiped out thousands of American farmers long before the 1929 crash. The elder Scruggs then found a job with a company that rented oil-drilling equipment and, during most of the 1920s, worked on projects in the Huasna Valley, the backcountry where pioneer Isaac Sparks had once lost an eye to a grizzly bear.

Jack's music lessons began about the time he was in the fifth grade at Arroyo Grande Elementary School—a school long gone, replaced by an automobile dealership—so he was nine or ten when he discovered the formidable talent that would bring him to the battleship USS *Arizona* and to a crossroads in American history. On a website that pays tribute to the ship's crew—1,177 died in the attack—Jack's younger sister, Pauline Scruggs Ellis, remembers a family that took naturally to music. Both parents sang. Jack's mother sang in the church choir and for weddings. Jack began his musical education on the piano and, at twelve, on the trombone.

It was, of course, a trombonist, Glenn Miller, whose big-band sound would help to lift the country out of the torpor of the Great Depression and whose

1944 disappearance over the English Channel would make him mythical but no more special than the 400,000 other young Americans taken away too abruptly and too soon.

The big bands enchanted Jack Scruggs, by the late 1930s a student in high school in Long Beach, where his family had moved in the years just before the war. He listened to swing records almost obsessively, fascinated by its structure, not just its sound. He was a sophisticated student of musical arrangement, and so, self-taught, he formed his own dance band.

Pauline discusses Jack's decision to enter the navy:

> *Along with all of the young men, Jack registered for the draft. He was not looking forward to serving in the army and, wanting to further his musical education, applied to the navy School of Music. He was accepted and looked forward to what he thought would be two years at the school and four years in the navy. Jack arrived at the school in December 1940 and was sent to Norfolk. After boot camp, he reported to the school to start his training of different musical subjects as well as private lessons on the piano and trombone. He played in the band and dance band. He soon sent home for his accordion and played that quite a bit since all the pianos were being taken off the ships.*[48]

In May 1941, the newly graduated U.S. Navy Band 22 left Norfolk to be assigned to the *Arizona*, the musicians doubtlessly excited at the prospect of a berth in Hawaii. According to the memoirs of battleship sailor Theodore Mason, a radioman on the *California*, they would have been disappointed. Sailors and other servicemen were treated like second-class citizens, and life on the capital ships based at Pearl Harbor was monotonous and oppressive.[49]

The navy knew that and provided antidotes: movies, sports—one poignant item recovered from the *Arizona*'s wreckage was a crew member's letterman's sweater with a huge block *A*—and music. In this, the battleship's band excelled. Champions in earlier competitions, it had defeated the Marine Corps band in the semifinals of the Pacific fleet's "Battle of the Bands" in November 1941, which doubtlessly gave every sailor on Battleship Row immense satisfaction.

Molly Kent, the sister of another bandsman and the author of the book *USS* Arizona's Last Band: The History of US Navy Band Number 22, writes that her brother and his friends would've been in the audience for another semifinal contest on December 6, both to check out the competition and to reunite with friends from the navy school of music who made up the battleship *Tennessee*'s band.[50]

Jack Scruggs was up early the next day. He was among a detachment assembling for the 8:00 a.m. colors ceremony and the national anthem.

The Japanese attack began at 7:55 a.m.

Scruggs was near the stern of the *Arizona* moments later, when the first bombs straddled the big ship. Lieutenant Commander Samuel G. Fuqua describes the moment in his after-action report:

> *I was in the ward room* [sic] *eating breakfast about 0755 when a short signal on the ship's air raid alarm was made. I immediately went to the phone and called the officer of the deck to sound general quarters and then shortly thereafter ran up to the starboard side of the quarterdeck to see if he had received word. On coming out of the wardroom hatch on the port side, I saw a Japanese plane go by, the machine guns firing, at an altitude of about 100 feet. As I was running forward on the starboard side of the quarterdeck, approximately by the starboard gangway, I was apparently knocked out by the blast of a bomb, which I learned later had struck the face plate of No. 4 turret on the starboard side and had glanced off and gone through the deck just forward on the captain's hatch, penetrating the decks and exploding on the third deck.*[51]

The photograph from an attacking plane shows that bomb's detonation—the concussion would kill three *Arizona* bandsmen instantly, blowing their bodies into the harbor. One of them was Jack Leo Scruggs, and this moment in time—the end of this gifted twenty-two-year-old's life—is frozen in the Japanese photo.

Jack's bandmates would live only moments longer. At the moment of their friend's death, they would have been on their way to or already at their general quarters action stations as ammunition loaders for the *Arizona*'s main armament, the fourteen-inch guns in the forward Number Two turret. The big guns, intended for the kind of ship-to-ship duel reminiscent of Nelson's navy, were useless in an air raid.

At 8:10 a.m., the fatal blow came only a few feet outboard from their turret. Dropped by Imperial Japanese Navy petty officer Noboru Kanai, a second 1,760-pound armor-piercing bomb penetrated the *Arizona*'s teak deck and detonated amid black powder charges that were used to power the ship's seaplane catapults. The black powder, in turn, triggered a massive chain reaction in the ship's magazine. The explosion that followed lifted the thirty-one-thousand-ton ship completely out of the water; it settled, heavy and twisted, with its tripod masts canted at surreal angles, and burned for two days.

Navy Band 22 was wiped out in that explosion. The burst of fire that accompanied it was so intense that a Naval Academy class ring was found fused to a bulkhead. The ring was all that remained of Rear Admiral Isaac J. Kidd, who flew his flag on the *Arizona*. Jack Scruggs, in a happier time, had played "Happy Birthday" on his accordion for Kidd's wife.[52]

News of the attack reached the people of Arroyo Grande at 11:30 a.m. This was a quiet time when they might have been listening to a light program of classical music on CBS while reading a Sunday paper from San Francisco or Los Angeles and waiting for the big lunch that, for many American families, was as traditional as Sunday church. For Juzo Ikeda's children, church would have meant services at Arroyo Grande First United Methodist, where, three years earlier, in a foreshadowing of the suffering that was to come, Japanese American members of the church had donated a painting of Christ in Gethsemane, struggling with the fear he felt as the Temple Guard was on its way to arrest him.[53]

It is said that many Americans had to find an atlas to locate Hawaii. In the first CBS bulletin, newsman Bob Trout pronounced the island where the *Arizona* burned, the *Oklahoma* capsized and 160 warplanes were destroyed on the ground as "Owahoo."

Will Tarwater, whose family ranched in the Huasna Valley and who spent a career as a border patrol agent and police officer—a career that you learn, once you get to know him, has deepened in him an innate sense of justice and compassion—remembers being in town with his father when they heard the news. They were "completely shocked," Will remembered. "It was beyond our understanding. Bewildered! We went home and turned on the radio to hear more. Still could not make any sense of it."[54]

A little more than an hour after the first radio broadcast, *San Luis Obispo Tribune* photographer and archivist David Middlecamp wrote, the fire siren in the county seat to the north of Arroyo Grande, affectionately called "Ferdinand," began to wail. This was the summons for Fortieth Division soldiers in training at Camp San Luis Obispo to return immediately to base. County sheriff Murray Hathaway dispatched extra deputies to Union Oil Company storage facilities on the other side of town; the company itself provided extra security for Avila Beach and Estero (Morro) Bay. The *Telegram-Tribune* rushed a Sunday edition to print when it became apparent that the Philippines were under attack, as

The high school on Crown Hill that the World War II generation knew, in a photo taken shortly before its demolition in the early 1960s. *Courtesy Randy Spoeneman.*

well.[55] Tarwater remembered both that Sunday edition and the size of its headlines seven decades later.

The next day, he and his classmates at Arroyo Grande Union High School gathered in their new gymnasium—a New Deal WPA work project that still serves as the Paulding Middle School gym today—to listen to Franklin Roosevelt's dramatic eight-minute address asking Congress for a declaration of war. By December 8, the initial disbelief that news of the attack generated had been replaced by growing fear. This is when the rumors began—rumors that Will Tarwater refused to believe since one of his closest friends was classmate Ben Dohi, a Japanese American. Tarwater recalled:

> *After Pearl Harbor, rumor mills had a heyday about it. All kinds of wild rumors about everything: a large farmhouse off Halcyon near the highway had a basement full of guns! Another house had a secret room full of short-wave radios and they were in constant contact with Tokyo...on and on. It seemed like someone was trying to turn us against our neighbors. Most of us couldn't buy it. We had grown up with them.[56]*

FBI agents descended on the valley that day to begin their field investigations, and they began to collect the heads of the farm families. Shigechika Kobara was an important target because of his leadership in the

Japanese American community. He would spend the following days in the county jail and then in army custody in North Dakota before being reunited with his family in the Arizona desert.[57] Juzo Ikeda would have faced the same fate, but he had broken his neck in a farm accident and was helpless, watched over by his wife, Sei, and his three sons.[58] The agents somehow missed another prominent man, Yeiju Hayashi, which was a relief to his fifteen-year-old son, Haruo, because it would be his father's stoic strength that would keep the family together in the months to come.

Haruo Hayashi, a sophomore at the high school in 1941, had grown up with three friends who meant everything to him: John Loomis, Gordon Bennett and Don Gullickson. They fished, bowled and played practical jokes that Tom Sawyer would have envied. Haruo, recovering from an appendectomy when he heard the news of the attack, dreaded his return to school a week later. He had no idea how he'd be received. But nothing had changed John, Gordon and Don. Three years later, all three were fighting the Japanese—Loomis as a marine and Bennett and Gullickson as sailors—but they also would write letters posted to his internment camp at Gila River, Arizona. Their friendship was a constant, but it was not universal. Haruo doesn't remember the names of the classmates who insulted him when he returned—they are not important to him. He does remember a tough Italian American kid, Milton Guggia, who told him: "I will personally beat the crap out of any kid who calls you a Jap."[59]

Years later, John Loomis, who fought on Peleliu and Okinawa, celebrated New Year's Eve with Haruo and his family. He sometimes would regale them with war stories, and one year, the former marine's frequent use of the term "Jap" grated on one of Haruo's sons, Alan, who began to turn red with anger. John was a tough but not insensitive man. He stopped his war story, looked at Alan with concern, and said, "Jesus Christ, Alan. You're not a Jap. You're an *American*."

But that distinction may have begun to blur two weeks after Pearl Harbor. The war arrived offshore. Verna Nagy was a young civilian employee at Camp San Luis Obispo. She lived in Shell Beach, a lovely seaside town five minutes north of Arroyo Grande, and was looking out her picture window for a picture-postcard view of the Pacific when she froze. The shaft of a submarine's periscope appeared where she might have preferred the spout of a migrating gray whale instead.[60] Farther north, a local cattlewoman had a different reaction. Many years later, she would tell Port San Luis Harbor commissioner Donald Ross that she'd seen a sub surface offshore during her shift on a volunteer shore patrol, somewhere along the beach in what is

The tanker *Montebello* was sunk off Cambria by the Japanese submarine *I-21*. *Courtesy Cambria Historical Society.*

today Montaña de Oro State Park. She let fly with her 30-30 carbine. The range was too great, she told Ross, but she had the satisfaction of seeing the crew scamper below and the captain dive the boat.[61]

They're plausible stories. The Imperial Japanese Navy had positioned nine submarines, or I-boats, all along the West Coast. One of them, *I-21* had, on the morning of December 22, fired a torpedo that missed its target, an oil tanker, off Point Arguello, about forty-five miles south of Arroyo Grande, and the submarine's captain, Kenji Matsumura, headed north in search of targets of opportunity. He would have passed Shell Beach on his way to another frustrating encounter, when his boat failed to sink the tanker *Larry Doheny* off the north coast of the county, despite an attack in which he fired another torpedo and opened fire with *I-21*'s deck gun.[62]

Matsumura found a third target in the little tanker *Montebello* off Cambria, but this time, the result was more satisfying for him. At 5:45 a.m. on December 23, he fired two torpedoes, and one hit; *I-21* surfaced and opened fire with its gun—its report could be heard inland by residents of Atascadero, twenty-six miles away—and although the *Montebello*'s crew escaped, the ship went under forty-five minutes after the attack had begun.

Within weeks, *I-21* was sinking ships off the Australian coast and shelled Sydney Harbor. Ultimately, the sub was lost with all hands near Tarawa in 1943. Matsumura and his crew are ample demonstration of why this is called a "world" war.

Three days after the *Montebello* sinking, the *Arroyo Grande Herald-Recorder* ran the story of Wayne Morgan's death on the *Arizona*.

So the surreal shock of Pearl Harbor, followed by the submarine attacks just off the California coast, generated a fear seen at its most extreme in the "Battle of Los Angeles" in February, where antiaircraft batteries, aided by an array of searchlights, opened fire on an air attack that never existed. Californians' fears far outweighed reason. In 1942, Japanese I-boats sunk four ships off the West Coast. At the same time, German U-boats sank seventy ships off North Carolina's Outer Banks alone, when Americans from Coney Island to Miami Beach could watch as doomed American merchantmen and their crews burned on the horizon.

Nevertheless, it was time, some began to say, to get the Japanese out—away, at least, from the coast, where they were suspected of Fifth Column activities like those in the wild rumors Will Tarwater had sense enough to doubt. When Mutual Broadcasting commentator John B. Hughes advocated the removal of the Japanese in a January 1942 broadcast, he was flooded with letters of support—but those letters revealed a different emotion entirely.

One came from a woman in Guadalupe, a little town just south of Arroyo Grande:

> *Today's* [broadcast] *really came close to home. We live near this small town where nearly one half are Japs. They farm all the best land and pay outrageous prices per acre, such as $45 or $50, and live in a shack to do it. Besides* [they] *own the theatre, half the garages and just about run this town…really, this is no country for such people.*

Two women from San Luis Obispo, north of Arroyo Grande, agreed. In a joint letter, they commended Hughes: "We want to congratulate you on the stand you are taking towards the Japs. We wish there were more like you. We have lived in and around San Luis Obispo all our lives and have seen enough of the Japs to know that our races can never mix."

A local businessman wrote, "I have talked to many people around the Arroyo Grande Valley…and the Japs farm two thirds of the best valley land and own 10% of it now, and every one of them are of the same opinion that now is the time to put the screws to the Japs before it is too late."

So many of the letters to Hughes, like these, demonstrate blatant racism or envy but fail to cite the Japanese as a threat to national defense. But it would not be long until, indeed, the screws were put to them.[63]

WORLD WAR II ARROYO GRANDE

The president of the United States would apply them in early 1942. Roosevelt's worldview had hardened even before Pearl Harbor, as historian Lynne Olson notes in her book about the president's bitter struggle with American isolationists, *Those Angry Days*. Britain's struggle to survive the Blitz, the immense shock of the December attacks, Churchill's deep depression generated by the February fall of Singapore to the Japanese, the efforts of a well-organized British lobby within the United States and, finally, the wiretaps he had authorized J. Edgar Hoover to place on enemy aliens all had, Olson suggests, a cumulative effect on the president's personality. He no longer saw shades of gray.[64]

On February 19, 1942, Franklin D. Roosevelt issued Executive Order 9066, which ordered the removal of all Japanese and Japanese Americans from the West Coast. Committed to defending the country, wounded by the devastation of his beloved navy's Pacific Fleet and bolstered by public opinion, Roosevelt overrode his own Justice Department, which disputed 9066's constitutionality, not to mention his First Lady, Eleanor, who disputed its humanity. The president ordered the Western Defense Command under General John Dewitt to begin removing "persons of Japanese ancestry."

FDR and his secretary of war, Henry Stimson, had picked the right man. DeWitt accepted his assignment with a sense of mission, and this is how he justified it: "In the war in which we are now engaged racial affinities are not severed by migration. The Japanese race is an enemy race and while many second and third generation Japanese born on United State soil, possessed of United States citizenship, have become 'Americanized,' the racial strains are undiluted."[65]

DeWitt now took control of the lives of 120,000 Pacific Coast residents—the 50,000 Issei, first-generation immigrants who were not allowed to become citizens under the Naturalization Act of 1790, a law repeatedly affirmed by the Supreme Court that restricted that privilege to whites, and 70,000 Nisei, the second generation, by birth American citizens.

When the evacuation order came to San Luis Obispo County, the Defense Command gave San Luis Obispo County residents, according to Pat Nagano, a resident of the county's north coast, ten days to put their affairs in order and dispose of their property. He remembered what we would call "yard sales" today, but these were sad little events where families tried to sell those possessions they couldn't store or take with them.[66] In South County, twenty-four-year-old Kazuo Ikeda, his father paralyzed by a farm accident, took charge of the family's one hundred acres, and he remembered

Buses arrive in Santa Maria, just south of Arroyo Grande, to evacuate Japanese families there. *Photo courtesy Corinne Kawaguchi.*

remorseless men, outsiders, who bought the family car and his father's trucks for pennies on the dollar.[67]

In April 1942, South County Japanese met waiting buses at the high school parking lot in Arroyo Grande, and there was a poignant moment when the Women's Club brought box lunches for their neighbors to take with them to the temporary assembly center in Tulare. The loaded buses then would've crept down Crown Hill in low gear, on their way to the two-lane 101 on the western edge of town, and their passengers, crammed inside with their luggage crammed in the bellies of the buses, would have rolled down Branch Street past familiar places: E.C. Loomis and Son, the Commercial Company market, F.E. Bennett's Grocery, Mr. Preuss's drugstore and Mr. Wilkinson's butcher shop, Buzz's Barber and Beauty, the Grande Theater, the Bank of America and, finally, the twin churches, Methodist and Catholic.

The Nisei children and teenagers who grew up here (of the fifty-eight seniors of the high school's class of 1942, twenty-five were on the buses) and had never known any other place did not know whether they would ever see these places again.

Many of them wouldn't.

Part of the ill-fated Arroyo Grande Union High School class of 1942. Mits Fukuhara would serve in an army tank unit; Lilly Fuchiwaki's family was close to the family of principal Clarence Burrell; and Barbara Gularte was the sister of two wartime combatants and the daughter of Joseph Gularte, the Corbett Canyon farmer who helped to pioneer strawberry cultivation in the area. *Courtesy Randy Spoeneman.*

Just past the churches, the drivers, with their silent passengers, turned north to make the connection for the long, colorless journey into the San Joaquin Valley.

Nearly seventy-five years later, Will Tarwater, who lives in Arizona, is still angry about what happened. The day the buses left was the kind of day an Arroyo Grande boy like Will would otherwise have enjoyed with friends like Ben Dohi—it was the day before trout season opened.

Not all Californians would be as charitable as the Arroyo Grande Women's Club or as outraged as Tarwater. Some would soon begin to loot vacant farms and farmhouses, and sometimes, in little farm towns throughout California, they would burn the houses, tractor sheds and barns after they had taken everything with the remotest value. After the war, Japanese Americans would seek redress from the federal government for property damage; the $37 million they would receive, after negotiating a bureaucratic maze, was a fraction of the actual loss.[68]

Typical was a local group of parents, represented by Hugh Dohi, who attempted to recover the rent it had lost and the utility and watchman's bills it had paid for the little Japanese-language school in Arroyo Grande. The parents sued to recover their loss in 1952. It took five years for the case to be decided. The parents asked for $1,230.00 in compensation; the Department of Justice awarded them $305.25.[69]

The school itself, on East Cherry Avenue, became a Boy Scout troop's headquarters after the war—until, in 2011, two teenagers, evidently for the thrill of watching it burn, set the building afire. It was a total loss. Mits Fukuhara's father had funded the school's construction in 1935.

"If my dad were here," Fukuhara said simply in the wake of the arson, "he'd be crying."[70]

CHAPTER 5

THE WAR IN EUROPE

The French have some swell farms here. Also, the French girls sure are pretty.
—William Carnes, April 24, 1943

In the "Letters from 'Our Boys'" column that Newell Strother published in the *Arroyo Grande Herald-Recorder*, Carnes sounds just like the country boy he really was. He marvels at a meal that was served to a buddy ("4 or 5 different kinds of wine and the same number of courses") by a French family while he conquered any fear of scary movies as his tank company was bivouacked in a cemetery overnight.

Ghosts and, even more, the bewildering array of North African insect life, including the mosquitoes and scorpions he ruefully describes, may have been Carnes's biggest worries in April 1943. The American army was then near the culmination of its first campaign against German and Italian forces, one that had begun with Operation Torch, the invasion of French North Africa, in November 1942. Three weeks before Carnes wrote his letter, General George Patton's Second Corps had defeated the famed *Afrika Korps* at El Guettar, Tunisia.

Carnes and GIs like him would have time to rest before the next big American action in the European Theater of Operations, Operation Husky, or the invasion of Sicily. Meanwhile, in preparation for the campaign against Hitler's Fortress Europe, other Arroyo Grande servicemen were gathering at airfields far to the north.

Among them was First Lieutenant Clarence Ballagh, a brilliant young man who'd been the 1936 Arroyo Grande Union High School valedictorian; he went on to Cal, where he earned a degree in engineering before the war came. Ballagh learned to copilot the B-17, or Flying Fortress, and he was assigned overseas duty at an airfield in Cambridgeshire, RAF Alconbury.[71]

B-17 pilots were extraordinary young men, but Ballagh was more extraordinary still. His unit was an experimental one, the 813th Squadron, 482nd Bomb Group, 8th Air Force. (Seventy-two B-17s made up a bomb group, each divided into four squadrons.) He and his squadron mates were to be "Pathfinders." Their planes were equipped with the new radar, installed in the chin of the aircraft, with a bulb of instruments replacing the ball

Clarence Ballagh as a Cal student. *Photo courtesy the Ballagh family.*

turret underneath. The bombers of the 813th would be the first in over a target. If the target was obscured by cloud cover—or so the theory proposed—it was up to the 813th to find it, deliver their bombs and then signal, by flare, the drop point for the trailing squadrons.[72]

Ballagh had the kind of mind that would've instantly grasped the technological potential for the Pathfinder's mission, but the danger of his assignment would be significant. The Eighth Air Force, by war's end, had sustained more combat deaths than the marines who'd attacked the Japanese head-on in the Central Pacific—about twenty-six to twenty-four thousand, respectively—and an airman's chances of completing the required twenty-five bombing missions were about one in four. In a study of one thousand Eighth Air Force missions in the summer of 1944, the U.S. Army's Office of Medical History—in clinical language that somehow makes the way fliers died even more horrific—revealed:

> *Approximately 86 percent of the casualties were hit by flak fragments. Less than 4 percent were hit by shells or shell fragments fired from enemy fighter planes. Practically all of the 7.8 percent of casualties hit by secondary*

missiles were the result of flak hits [antiaircraft fire] *on the aircraft. Secondary missiles include fragments of Plexiglas; pieces of dural from the skin of, or objects in, the plane; bulletproof glass; brass fittings; and parts of electrical heating and radio equipment and .50 caliber machinegun ammunition.*[73]

Ballagh's chances of surviving twenty-five missions would have been even lower than the average since his ship and his squadron would lead the other bombers of the 482nd into the target. They would have the full attention of both the flak guns and the superb German fighter aircraft. Ballagh was two weeks away from his first mission when he decided to hitch a ride north to Scotland, perhaps for the distraction that a short leave in Edinburgh could provide. The B-17 in which he rode had an unfortunate name—the *Flaming Maybe*—and an even more unfortunate pilot. The ship ran into heavy weather on its way north, and its pilot, new to flying on instruments, flew his airplane into the side of Mount Skiddaw in the Lake District. There were no survivors. Ballagh's body was brought home to Arroyo Grande for burial; skeletal fragments of *Flaming Maybe* remain on Mount Skiddaw today.[74]

Other Arroyo Grande fliers would survive the war but not before their status caused much anxiety back home. In March 1944, the *Herald-Recorder* reported that Lieutenant Ed Horner, a B-17 navigator, was missing after

"Flaming Maybe's" wreckage, on Mount Skiddaw, today. *Photo courtesy Ian Burgess and aircrashsites.co.uk.*

a massive series of raids over Germany known as "Big Week." Horner's mother would have received a curt telegram informing her that her son was missing in action, but two happier ones would follow. The first, after several weeks, informed her that Ed had survived and was a prisoner of war; the second, a year later, restored her son to her. The camp had been liberated, and Ed would soon be on his way home.

The average age of a World War II B-17 pilot was twenty-two; gunners were around eighteen. Elliott Whitlock was a twenty-two-year-old copilot in a B-17G assigned to the 377th Squadron of the Ninety-sixth Bomb Group, based at RAF Snetterton Heath in Norfolk. His father owned the Commercial Co. Market, located in the building that now houses a restaurant at the corner of Branch and North Mason Streets.

Besides Whitlock and the visiting Yanks, another resident of Snetterton Heath was a small donkey that the squadron adopted and christened "Lady Moe, Queen of the Heath." Her young admirers played baseball at the Lady Moe Ball Park and watched movies at the Lady Moe Theater. She had unlimited visiting privileges; some say she even flew a combat mission. She liked American cigarettes—that is, she liked eating them.

Lady Moe reciprocated the affection lavished on her. She began to appear with the ground crews at the control tower, waiting with

Lady Moe, the "Queen of the Heath," with a young 377th Squadron lieutenant. *Courtesy the American Air Museum in Britain.*

them while they anxiously counted B-17's as her boys returned from their missions.[75]

Moe almost lost Whitlock during the twenty-fourth of his twenty-five combat missions, a raid on Berlin in March 1944. The young copilot recounted the story of that mission in a letter home:

We had bombed the target and had started back when fire broke out in the cockpit so furiously I thought the plane would blow up any minute. Flares were blowing up and shells were going off.

The pilot, Jim Lamb, gave the order to bail out and then the intercommunicating phone went out. Our engineer and bombardier (Cliff) and navigator (Charley) bailed out over German territory.

At that time Jim's parachute caught fire as did an extra one we carried. Mine was burnt but not seriously. With his chute gone, Jim couldn't jump. I decided to stay with the ship while Jim put out the fire. He succeeded in getting it under control, but his hands were so badly burnt that he couldn't do anything the rest of the trip.

He held the ship level while I finished putting the fire out...Somebody handed a fire extinguisher through a hole the fire had burnt, and so I looked back and everybody was there (in the tail) for which I thanked God. Nobody...had bailed out. They had not heard the order.

...I had dived the ship immediately after the fire so that nobody would pass out if the oxygen was cut off. Suddenly we started to get an awful lot of flak (anti-aircraft fire from the ground) so I had to hurry back to the cockpit to do some evasive action which worked OK, incidentally. I had one of the boys get the maps...and had the radio operator get fixes so I plotted a course for home with as little flak as possible. The radio operator did a fine job so we came out on course and landed OK. All this was above the clouds, so I think I can qualify for navigator now as well as pilot...

...Your prayers are standing by me. I was praying up there and all the rest of the men were praying, too...

Lots of love,
Elliott[76]

Whitlock's conduct that day would earn him a Silver Star. A few weeks later, the same B-17, with a new crew, was shot down over the Pas-de-Calais. The tail gunner was the only survivor.[77]

Whitlock did survive, and after the war, he became an attorney, earning his law degree at the University of Southern California and then practicing

A B-17 from Elliott Whitlock's Ninety-sixth Bomb Group with at least one engine on fire begins to plunge to earth over Berlin, 1944. *National Archives.*

in San Bernardino County. At the time of his death, more than sixty years after that twenty-fourth mission, a local bar journal praised his wisdom and his kindness; he'd become a mentor to many young lawyers. He had led a good and important life.

How did the Brits feel about Yanks like Elliott Whitlock? They were, as the saying went, "overpaid, overfed, over-sexed, and over here." But there was something else the British felt, too. In 2005, they opened a little museum in a Quonset hut near the old airfield so that future generations could have the chance to know Elliott and his young friends. And before that, there was the figure incorporated into a stained-glass window of the local parish church. It would be reasonable to expect a traditional image: an angel, for example, looking earthward to proclaim Christ's birth. There is, instead, an American in his flight suit, looking heavenward, toward a risen Christ. The window is a poignant reminder of the constancy of the people of Norfolk, who had come to love the boys and men who made little Lady Moe their queen.

Jess Milo McChesney's family had flying in their blood—the San Luis Obispo airport is named for an elder brother, aviator Leo McChesney. The family owned a dairy on land between Arroyo Grande and San Luis Obispo and had opened, before the war, an insurance agency in San Luis Obispo. When the

B-24s from the Fifteenth Air Force, which included Jess Milo McChesney's Bomb Group, over the Ploesti oilfields. *National Archives.*

war came, Milo followed his brother's lead, and he, too, became a flier. He enlisted in May 1942 and completed flight training at La Junta, Colorado, in early 1943. Afterward, granted a seventy-two-hour leave, he flew his plane home to visit his folks. McChesney then learned to fly the B-24 Liberator, a heavy bomber, and he was sent to Italy in 1944.

In McChesney's first mission in June, the target was obscured by cloud cover. That might have been a blessing. McChesney and his crew, part of the 513th Squadron, 376th Bomb Group, 15th Air Force, were to attack the oil refineries in Ploesti, Romania, a target that was protected by two hundred fighters and nearly 150 antiaircraft guns. While on a parallel mission over another target that day, the 15th lost four B-17s, five B-24s and four fighter escorts to dense flak and swarms of German fighters, but the 513th was ordered home.[78]

McChesney wasn't off the hook—he had twenty-four more combat missions that covered most of southern Europe. The B-24s would return to Ploesti and hit other targets in Yugoslavia, Hungary, Germany and France, including the U-boat pens in Toulon and missions preparatory to Operation Dragoon, the invasion of southern France, in August 1944. An officer in another B-24 in McChesney's squadron recorded one of those missions in his diary:

[We hit the] *beaches of Southern France as cover for invasion. Whole 15ᵗʰ Air Force took part. Took off during the night. Saw plane #42 Blow up at end of runway. All men were killed. Seven planes of the 47ᵗʰ wing blew up that night saw one other one blow up. Beachhead was covered by clouds, and we got there a few seconds too late to drop our 40 hundred pounders. Saw all kinds of planes. B-26 - 25 - 17 - dive bombers - Hellcats - etc. No flak and no fighters at all. We had been scheduled to fly #42.*[79]

McChesney and his crew dodged a tragic ending like the seven Liberators in the mission over southern France when, on his last mission, he had to crash-land his damaged plane at a British airfield in Italy. The crew survived, with one member seriously injured, but McChesney's war was over. After stateside duty, he was discharged as a captain and returned, anticlimactically, to the insurance agency at 1016 Court Street in San Luis Obispo.[80]

A few months after McChesney's last mission over France, an infantryman, a more recent arrival to Arroyo Grande, found himself

The *President Pierce* brought Sadami Fujita to the West Coast; here it is passing the San Francisco–Oakland Bay Bridge while it is under construction. *Courtesy the Hawaii Aviation Preservation Society.*

fighting there. In October 1944, in Alsace, this soldier fought with the 442nd Regimental Combat Team, and he would win the Bronze Star while serving with this, the most decorated unit of its size in American military history, made up of Japanese Americans from the West Coast and Hawaii.

Sadami Fujita was born and raised in Hawaii. In 1939, at twenty-seven, he left Hawaii for California on the liner *President Pierce* with a younger brother, Jimmy. *Pierce* had already had its brush with history. It was intimately tied to the career of Amelia Earhart. It was one of the dozens of ships, both military and civil, that searched fruitlessly for the lost flier in 1937. But in 1934, *Pierce* had saved Earhart's life on her Hawaii-to-California flight in her beloved Lockheed Vega. From an account of that flight:

> *In the final hours of the journey Earhart found herself surrounded by a thick blanket of fog. Glancing down through a hole in the fog, she suddenly caught sight of a ship. She dove down through the hole, she wrote later, "faster than I ever flew before from 8,000 feet to 200!" The ship was the* President Pierce, *outward bound from San Francisco. Earhart lined her plane up with the wake of the ship and headed for California—now only 300 miles away!*[81]

By the 1940 census, Sadami Fujita, too, had found a home in California. He was living with Jimmy and another brother, Dick, in Arroyo Grande. The page from their district in that year's census is like a who's who of local farmers. It includes the Ikedas, the Hayashis, the Fukuharas and Javier Pantaleon, the foreman at the Waller Seed Co. to whom a doomed sailor named Felix Estibal wrote one of his last letters before being killed in action near Guadalcanal in November 1942.

Five months after FDR reinstated the draft, the U.S. Army tapped Sadami on the shoulder and, not unusual in the army, spelled his name wrong, "S DAMI FUJITA."[82] He was assigned to the 100th Infantry Battalion, a tough outfit made up of Hawaiian Japanese Americans, which was later merged with the 442nd Regimental Combat Team as that unit's First Battalion.[83] After months of costly combat in Italy, the 442nd was transferred to France in the fall of 1944. They went into action three days after arriving, in an attack on a rail center at a town called Bruyeres, but it was a rescue mission two weeks later that proved to be one of the most famous, and costly, of the unit's exploits.

The 1st Battalion of the 141st infantry, part of a prewar Texas National Guard division, had been cut off and surrounded by German troops in

Two soldiers from B Company, 100th Infantry Battalion—later merged into the 442nd Regimental Combat Team—in training. The soldier on the left in this photograph is identified only as "Fujita," but his height and physical build suggest it may be Private Sadami Fujita. *Courtesy the 100th Infantry Battalion Veterans Education Center, Masami Hamakado Collection.*

Soldiers from the 442nd Regimental Combat Team move up to the front in the Vosges Mountains, October 1944. *National Archives.*

rugged territory in the Vosges Mountains. Thanks to attrition, the 141st was largely made up, by 1944, of terrified nineteen-year-old draftees. On October 26, the Nisei soldiers were ordered to penetrate German lines to relieve the Texans. It took five days of what amounted to repeated head-on assaults by the 442nd, at tremendous cost. The Germans were well dug in, the Americans were exposed and, for the 141st infantry, the situation was increasingly desperate. By October 28, P-47 fighters were hazarding a barrage of fire—one was shot down—in attempting to drop supplies to the Texans by air. Later that day, American 155-mm artillery launched a barrage of shells, containing chocolate bars, wound tablets and field dressings, that fell on the 141st. It was on the twenty-eighth that Fujita was killed in the relief of what was being called the "Lost Battalion"; the breakthrough finally came on October 30.[84]

Enemy artillery fire killed many of the 442nd's men and might have killed Sadami during their relief efforts. The Germans fired 88-mm shells into the treetops, and as was the case in the Hurtgen Forest—a ferocious battle being fought at the same just inside Germany—many GIs were killed by flying splinters. Another possibility—perhaps a stronger one, given the Bronze Star Fujita won posthumously—was that he was among a group of volunteers bringing up more ammunition. They did so under intense small-arms fire, and many of them died in the attempt.[85]

In the end, at least 800 Nisei soldiers were killed or wounded to rescue the 230 Texans. The veterans resented their losses, and they resented the commanding officer of their Thirty-sixth Infantry Division, John E. Dahlquist, who seemed prone to ordering the unit into the kind of frontal attacks that proved so costly.

Hawaiian historian Duane Vachon writes tellingly of Dahlquist when he notes that, after the relief of the "Lost Battalion," the general ordered a review of the 442nd; only twenty men from Company K fell in. When Dahlquist rounded on a subordinate and demanded to know what was going on, the officer replied simply: "That's all of Company K that's left, sir." They had gone in with four hundred men. Years later, at Fort Bragg,

A color guard from the 442nd Regimental Combat Team during an awards ceremony shortly after their relief of the "Lost Battalion." *National Archives.*

a former commander of the 442nd, Lieutenant Colonel Gordon Singles, received General Dahlquist on a visit. He saluted. When the general extended his hand, in a gesture to "let bygones be bygones," Singles refused the handshake.[86]

After the war, Fujita was brought home—far away from the bitter cold of the Vosges Mountains—and lies today in the Punch Bowl, the American military cemetery on Oahu. In a cruel turn of events, the men who served with him had left home to fight for a nation that, thanks to Executive Order 9066, had left them homeless.

Missing home is a constant theme in letters written by local soldiers who were fighting the war in Europe.

Homer Edgecomb was a GI in Italy. He wrote of the beauty of the Italian countryside and the "happy, hard-working" farmers he saw and described the stark contrast soldiers encountered in towns that had been blasted by bombardment, the Darwinian struggle for food among the townspeople. Then he admitted feeling a little let down by his visit to Rome: "Right now I'd rather see Arroyo Creek than the Tiber River, Mt. Lassen rather than Vesuvius, and the grammar school porch would appeal to me a lot more than Mussolini's balcony—and I'll take a ride through the Huasna any day in preference to the Appian Way."

William Carnes, in North Africa, wrote:

I just saw one of the swellest sights. You will never believe it when I tell you. It was fresh green peas in a field…if you had been where we were and as long as we were, you would know why we thought so much of seeing a field of vegetables. We saw many wonderful sights…We saw country that reminded me of the Cuyama, some places reminded me of the scenery between San Simeon and Monterey. For the past few months we have seen nothing but country like that at Devils' Den, except there is more wind and sand here.

Carnes goes on to write about "some places where deer would thrive. Hillsides of brush, lots of oaks, creeks and water holes," all sights typical of the Arroyo Grande Valley, as are the trout he sees in some of the water holes, the doves he sees like the ones boys hunt in the valley, and he takes a moment off from his war to marvel at a treasure he discovers: a nest of quail eggs.

Some soldiers longed for a more tangible connection to home. Private Francis Fink, a jazz musician who formed a band after the war, just as the *Arizona* sailor Jack Scruggs had before the war, fought in France, and he wrote to his mother, Frances:

You can tell the editor of the Herald-Recorder *that I would like very much to get the paper. The first chance you get, I wish you would take out a subscription for me…*[to] *send me some of those flashlights that you can get down at Don's* [Variety Store]. *You can have Fritz do that for you. Also stick in a few candy bars.*

Other soldiers seemed to realize this might be their only chance to see such faraway places. Private First Class Kenneth Juler, in a letter to Mae Ketchum of Arroyo Grande:

We were in Naples the morning after Vesuvius erupted. That was a great sight, to see that smoke curling up into the air to great heights. I shouldn't say curling. I should say billowing. It was fully 20,000 to 25,0000 feet in the sky…The night scene was the magnificent and gorgeous one. The red hot molten lava was flowing down the sides in all directions and boiling over the top of the crater. The whole mountain was an orange-red outline…

Second Lieutenant Virginia Campondonico began a cheery letter:

Well, here I am in France. Are you surprised?
We have been talking French to the natives. We don't get along so good, but I guess it will be alright [sic] *in time. The first Frenchman to whom I said "Bonjour!" ("good morning" in French) answered me in good English. Did we laugh!…Dottie and I were talking this A.M. to a Frenchman who gave us some onions which we made into sandwiches with crackers and cheese. He also gave us a big bouquet of roses.*

Herman Petker, recovering in a British hospital from trench foot, was granted a little furlough time. He wrote to his parents that he loved his trip to Scotland, including Edinburgh, and indicated, in no uncertain terms, that he preferred the company of Scots to that of the English—he was even unimpressed with some English VIPs: "While I was on my furlough, I got to see the King and Queen and their daughter. They don't look any different than anybody else. I also got a chance to see the Scotsmen marching down the street playing the bagpipes. They were dressed in kilts…I surely had a good time."

Another convalescing soldier, Lieutenant Rea Pyle Jr., was sitting alongside his bed when an elegantly dressed, stately woman quietly pardoned herself. Pyle looked up as she extended her hand. She and her husband, she told him, wanted to host an American soldier for the weekend. Would he be interested? Pyle indicated he would, and within twenty-four hours, he was sipping 160-year-old brandy with her husband, a duke who insisted on being addressed in the familiar: "Call me Guy!" he jovially told Pyle when they met.

In the winter of 1944–45, Pyle's brandy would've been a godsend for GIs still on the front lines. This, too, was the same winter when Hitler launched *Nordwind*, the massive offensive that would be his last on the western front, repulsed in the Battle of the Bulge. None of the letters home come close—nor would army censors *allow* soldiers to come close—to capturing the kind of suffering GIs endured that winter. The censors were ruthless, as demonstrated by Arroyo Grande private first class Orval Rong, writing to his parents from New Guinea in 1944:

> *The censor says I can't say much,*
> *Can't talk of so and so and such and such.*
> *Can't even saying we're having weather,*
> *Or you'd put two and two together.*
> *Can't say where I am or what.*
> *Can't tell you if, or why, or but.*
> *Can't tell you what we do, or don't.*
> *But I can send my love to you*
> *Without restrictions. Which I do.* [87]

A more detailed picture of soldiering emerged after the war, thanks to accounts written by infantrymen, tankers and fliers who survived combat in the European Theater. In one of the most clear-eyed and sympathetic accounts of a "dogface's" life in Europe, *Roll Me Over*, written by Sergeant Raymond Gantter, the most vivid impression is not one of violence, which is infrequent, quick, overwhelming and merciless, but of constant discomfort. Gantter and his comrades were cold, wet and frequently hungry—a day could go by with little more than what was called hardtack in the Civil War—and bone-crushingly exhausted. It was a luxury for a soldier to be able to take off his shoes; a shave and a shower, weeks apart, must have been nearly a religious experience.

Gantter, like many soldiers, brought home a measure of survivor's guilt—particularly in one action, in a German town, when he ordered up tank support for his rifle squad. Two appeared and moved forward, and then one of them lazily turned off the road leading into the town; rolled slowly through a field, trailing thin, oily black smoke; and came to a muddy stop at

Frank and Sally Gularte at home enjoying a family barbecue, 1944. This may have been the last time they were together. *Courtesy Annie Gularte Silva.*

an embankment. Gantter suspected—and he was right—that the crew was dead. And they had died because he called for them.[88]

This was not Gantter's fault, of course. The fact that so many soldiers died in absurd ways, died due to mistakes in the execution of orders or the stupidity of the officer who issued them or died simply because of bad luck—none of this suggests that their lives meant nothing. Frank Gularte, the son of Azorean immigrants, the young man who worked at the E.C. Loomis feed store before the war, drafted into the army the summer before Pearl Harbor, left behind an irreplaceable gap for his wife, Sally, and for his baby son.

Gularte's unit, the 607th Tank Destroyer Battalion, attached to the 90th Infantry Division, had seen a lot of action. Originally organized at Fort Ord, outside Monterey, Frank would have some good luck. The unit did much of its training at Hunter Liggett, in southern Monterey County, or at Camp San Luis Obispo, both places close to home. So his visitors included his mother, Clara Gularte, and his six sisters, who also visited their brother Manuel, an artilleryman based at Camp Roberts in the north county.

In the spring of 1944, the entire family were together and intact for the last time at a barbecue on the Gularte ranch, off Corbett Canyon Road. Shortly after, the tank destroyer battalion shipped out. They landed on Utah Beach eleven days after D-day. A detachment was assigned almost immediately to provide support to the assault on Cherbourg, in the fighting that had been the first hard work done by Domingo Martinez's Seventy-ninth Infantry Division.

For the summer and fall, the 607th—its main armament at this point a three-inch gun towed by a half-track, or three-quarter-ton truck—sprinted across France under the command of perhaps the most famous American combat general. The battalion was part of George Patton's Third Army and so was undoubtedly infused with Patton's fighting spirit. Patton wanted his tanks and trucks infused, not just his men, and in his drive during the breakout from Normandy—the grand chase across France that Domingo Martinez would not live to see—he wasn't hesitant about sending details back to Omaha Beach to steal entire gasoline supply companies for the Third Army's use. My father, a quartermaster officer in London, was responsible for sending those units to the beachhead.

Their absence one day led to what had to be the most extravagantly profane cross-Channel phone call ever placed. An irate divisional commander on Omaha Beach bellowed that Lieutenant Gregory would be Private Gregory within twenty-four hours and added that there wasn't a foxhole in northern France deep enough to protect him from the enemy artillery bombardment

A column from the 607th Tank Destroyer Battalion uses a pontoon bridge to ford a German river about eight weeks after Frank Gularte was killed in action. *National Archives.*

that the general would be happy to arrange. My father got off the hook when the gasoline's disappearance was traced to Third Army.

The Americans' breakout from Normandy, after claustrophobic weeks in the death traps of the hedgerows, must have been a jubilant one, but the 607th would encounter another death trap whose brutality sobered them. The Americans, under Omar Bradley, and the British and Canadians, under Bernard Law Montgomery, had the chance to encircle the entire German army in Normandy. They failed, and thousands of Germans—battle-weary, some of them now barefoot, running for their lives along narrow roads and cattle trails through what became known as the Falaise Gap—escaped.[89]

But American artillery units still found many of them there—artillery spotters were nearly incoherent because there were so many targets to call in on their field radios—and the slaughter they inflicted was horrific. Seventy years later, one of the 607th's soldiers, Frank Kunz, remembered the results in an interview with his hometown newspaper: "Christ help me. There were 6 to 8 inches of bodies and horses ground up on the road. There was nothing you could do. You had to drive through it." People, Kunz added, don't understand what war is.[90]

Patton's chase ended in September on the Moselle River at the old Roman garrison town of Metz. It took him two months to break down German resistance, and Gularte's 607th, attached to the 95th Infantry Division, fought in several actions around the city. In one of them, a company of the unit was credited with firing the first Third Army shells into Germany, aimed at a church steeple in the town of Perl.

By November 23, the battalion was fighting along the river, six miles south of Metz. The Moselle, beautiful, calm and, in summer, a soft blue, might have made Gularte homesick if he'd had the opportunity to see it then, in peace. The river's surface is punctuated by ringlets as trout nose up to feed, and in the long twilight hours of summer nights, little French boys do what little boys in the Arroyo Grande Valley do—they go fishing.

But with winter descending in 1944, it was along the Moselle where the unit saw one of its finest hours. Company C, unsupported by infantry, was charged with holding a little town, Falck. By this time, the 607th had made the important transition from a towed to a self-propelled unit. Its main anti-tank weapon was a robust 90-mm gun—with its armor-piercing shell, it was a match for the German 88—mounted on a tank chassis. This was the M36. C Company, commanded by First Lieutenant George King, came under mortar and artillery fire and then repeated infantry assaults from the woods, still dense around the town today. The enemy wanted Falck back, but it would not get it. Smith's tank destroyers and their crews alone would turn them back in their repeated assaults, and the young officer would earn a Silver Star for his leadership that day, November 27, 1944.

That was Frank Gularte's last full day of life. On the twenty-eighth, the 607th was ordered to take another town, Merten. Everything that could go wrong did. The infantry that was to support the big M36s never materialized. The 3rd Platoon of Company C took on Merten by itself. The first M36 to advance down the road was fired on and returned fire, but then, in moving around a tank barrier, it got mired in the mud and so was easily destroyed by a German anti-tank crew. The next destroyer turned back, the third tumbled into a ditch and was set ablaze by enemy fire and the fourth's gun jammed. When it turned to return to Falck, this last destroyer, too, became bogged down in the mud.[91] Somewhere in the mêlée, a German sniper took the life of the young man who would never see his son.[92]

Only five days later, Sally Gularte gave birth to Frank Jr. A few days after that—after she'd first held her son close in her arms—she received the War Department telegram that informed her of her husband's death.

The squad leader/writer, Sergeant Gantter, wrote of a young man in his company who carried, from his arrival in France to the German frontier, a box of cigars to share once he had word of the birth of his first child. Gantter liked the young man: he was earnest, friendly and desperate for word from home. But mail was slow—Gantter shared Christmas cookies with his fellow dogfaces in March—so the young soldier eventually gave up the waiting and gave out his cigars when the due date had safely come and gone. Gularte must have been waiting anxiously for word from home, as well—receiving it would be a joyful distraction from the filth, the cold and the constant, dull exhaustion—and it would be a sign, too, that there was a new reason to survive the war, a new reason to get himself home.

Many at home, and in the front lines in Europe, as well, according to Gantter, hoped the war would be over by Christmas. The chase across France had given both false hopes. It would instead be a hard Christmas—hard in the Ardennes, with the onslaught of *Nordwind*, the great German offensive, and hard, too, for the Gularte family. On Wednesday, December 13, Father Thomas Morahan celebrated a Mass at St. Patrick's Church in Frank's memory.[93]

Even then, the war would not leave the family alone. Four days later, Frank's brother, Manuel, and his 965th Field Artillery Battalion began a desperate fight around St. Vith, Belgium, in support of the 7th Armored Division, charged with holding the town as the Battle of the Bulge began. The Americans would lose the town to the Germans, but the 965th's heavy guns—155-mm howitzers—would be one of the factors that would make them pay dearly for it, wrecking, in the process, the *Wehrmacht*'s timetable. The 7th Armored abandoned St. Vith, but only after holding on for a full four days past the German target date, December 17, for its seizure.[94]

That was the day that the 101st Airborne Division arrived to take up defensive positions in and around Bastogne, Belgium. Their stubborn resistance in holding this town, in the rear of the German advance, was another decisive factor that prevented the Bulge from becoming the breakthrough that Hitler so desperately wanted. The German drive to the west lost momentum as thousands of *Wehrmacht* soldiers were thrown into the attack on Bastogne. There, among the tough and battle-wise Americans—some of their foxholes are faintly visible today—was a paratrooper from Arroyo Grande, Arthur C. Youman. December 17 was his twenty-third birthday.[95]

Paratroopers of the 101ˢᵗ Airborne moving out of Bastogne on December 29, 1944, for a counterattack on the Germans who surrounded them for nine days. *National Archives.*

Youman was Kentucky born and was raised in Kern County, but he'd been living in Arroyo Grande when he enlisted in 1943. He and his comrades were told that the 101ˢᵗ faced, at most, three days in the line. It didn't work out that way. For nine days, they were surrounded, relying on scattered airdrops of food and ammunition to keep going. George Patton's 3ʳᵈ Army launched a furious attack on the southern shoulder of the Bulge and finally broke through. The first of Patton's tankers to make contact with the 101ˢᵗ, on December 26, was Creighton Abrams, the future commander of American forces in Vietnam. But German resistance continued, with Youman and the paratroopers fighting into February, when they were finally pulled off the line. They had, in the meantime, endured not just the last great German offensive of the war but also the coldest winter in Europe in thirty years.

Youman was a good soldier in one of the best combat units in American military history. He'd dropped into Normandy on D-day, helped capture the key Norman town Carentan and then joined the 101ˢᵗ in the ill-conceived Operation Market Garden—Field Marshal Montgomery's attempt to seize the Rhine River bridges in Holland and deliver a thrust into Germany. Market

Arthur Youman, second from left, with fellow Easy Company paratroopers during training in South Carolina. *Courtesy Michel de Trez and the D-Day Paratroopers Historical Center, Saint-Come-du-Mont, Normandy.*

Garden was a fiasco, and it would claim another Arroyo Grande paratrooper, Lieutenant Francis Eberding, a member of the 82nd Airborne Division.[96]

The 101st fought in Holland from September until the end of October. One high point came when Youman's company rescued one hundred British soldiers stranded near Arnhem, the centerpiece for Cornelius Ryan's *A Bridge Too Far*. It was immediately after Market Garden that Youman would be promoted to sergeant; he'd impressed his boss. The young officer who promoted him was Lieutenant Richard Winters, the commander of Easy Company, 506th Parachute Infantry Regiment, 101st Airborne Division. Youman was one of historian Stephen Ambrose's "Band of Brothers."[97]

CHAPTER 6

THE INTERNEES' WAR

In 1942, the Nakamura family were among the passengers in the little fleet of buses that left the high school parking lot on Crown Hill. They were among the first arrivals at the newly opened relocation center, the Tulare Assembly Center. At its largest, this temporary camp housed five thousand internees until a permanent camp was ready. Constructed on a site that had been used for the county fair before the war, there was space for them there, even though it meant sleeping in the stinking animal stalls.

What happened at this place in the space of five months is extraordinary. The Tulare camp produced a newspaper, the remarkable *Tulare News*, that buzzed with news from the schools established there and featured advice columns and an extended sports section.[98] The sport section included many stories written by George Nakamura, who, along with his brother, had played on Vard Loomis's baseball team and had been a sports reporter on his Arroyo Grande high school paper, the *Hi-Chatter*.

The young people who had been members of the high school's class of 1942 received a visitor that spring. It was their principal, Clarence Burrell. Burrell was close to the Japanese community, and especially to the Fuchiwaki family. One of the Fuchiwakis' daughters, Helen, worked at the high school where her younger siblings were students, and she cared for two of Burrell's children—Souya, six, and Peter, three. When the government announced that the West Coast Japanese would be removed, Burrell asked his teachers to accelerate the programs of the Japanese American seniors so that they could graduate on time. Two months after his students had been taken away, Burrell

Arroyo Grande Union High School principal Clarence Burrell personally delivered diplomas to his class of 1942 students who had been interned. *Author's collection.*

drove to Tulare to personally present them with their high school diplomas.[99]

The *Tulare News* published thirty-two editions between May and August 1942, and the farewell edition included a heartfelt letter of thanks from the assembly center's Nils Aanonsen, a compassionate man who defied the army and allowed the camp to elect its own leadership. An article paints an optimistic picture, thanks to accounts in travel magazines, about their ultimate destination. That was a camp at Gila River, Arizona. When Nakamura and his family arrived and he saw what a desolate place it was, the first thing he did was get out. Determined to prove his loyalty, he joined the army.

George Nakamura's army aptitude tests immediately impressed the brass. He was brilliant, and he knew Japanese—his skill would be sharpened at military language school in Minnesota—so he became an army intelligence specialist. After combat training with the 442nd Regimental Combat Team, he commanded, despite his youth, a group of four GIs assigned to what the army called the "Dixie Mission." In 1944, Sergeant Nakamura and his team were inserted into the mountains of Shaanxi province in central China, where they assisted Chinese guerrillas in intelligence gathering as they resisted the imperial Japanese army and its brutal counterintelligence arm, the *kempeitai*, or the military police.

From his base with a group of Chinese resistance fighters, Nakamura and his fellow Americans joined on intelligence-gathering missions. Nakamura acted as translator in the interrogation of Japanese soldiers captured on some of them, but on one mission, he went alone. He would win the Bronze Star for the daring rescue of a downed American pilot.[100]

Sergeant George Nakamura during intelligence and language training in Minnesota, 1943. *Photo courtesy the Nakamura family.*

His Chinese hosts in their remote camp grew to like this Arroyo Grande soldier so much that, on his twenty-first birthday, they threw him a party. There were toasts and even a little dancing. One of the soldiers, a young woman named Jiang, took a turn dancing with Nakamura. They tried, perhaps, a fox trot. She had been an actress before the war and so was a woman of culture.

The young American officer would, after the war, get his master's degree in international relations from Columbia University, which

Jiang Qing on the cover of a 1935 movie magazine. *From Wikimedia Commons, public domain.*

suggests the kind of sophistication that might have made him a good dance partner.

His partner, Jiang, was married to an influential husband and was powerful in her own right, but she would be reviled someday—in fact, in the many twists and turns that twentieth-century Chinese history took, the last two decades turned against Jiang. In 1981, the Communist government put her on trial for her life, in a courtroom where she was repeatedly mocked and insulted. In the peculiar Chinese dialect that is the language of the Party, she became the "White-Boned Demon."

Jiang, in return, was defiant and supremely contemptuous of her accusers. She was fully aware that she was the star of a televised version of what was essentially a Stalinist show trial, and she was determined to do a star turn. Her fiery defense was irrelevant, of course, and Jiang was sentenced to be executed. Jiang was by now a widow, but her deceased husband still held enough sway that she was not shot. The court instead handed down a life sentence for her membership in the "Gang of Four," those accused of helping to conceive and carry out the disastrous 1968 Cultural Revolution. She would commit suicide in prison in 1991.

For almost forty years before that ignominious end to her long life, Jiang was known universally by what was essentially her stage name in a role she

Former congressman and transportation secretary Norman Mineta with George Nakamura (center) and his son, Gary (right), in 2009. *Photo courtesy the Nakamura family.*

relished more than any other and what was easily the role of a lifetime. George Nakamura's dance partner on his twenty-first birthday had been Madame Mao Zedong.

Nakamura would live a long life, too, but his would be a happier one. He finished his army career in Japan, where he served, after the war, as an interpreter for MacArthur's occupation; some call this period the vainglorious general's shogunate, after the three-hundred-year military dictatorship of the Tokugawa clan. (After the Tokugawa era, the ancestors of Arroyo Grande's Japanese Americans had begun to come to America.)

The course of Nakamura's life would take him in the opposite direction. After finishing Columbia, he returned to Japan, where he lived for thirty years in Tokyo as the East Asian manager of a large American electronics firm and as the head of a management consulting company. He and his wife retired to Hawaii and then moved to Texas to be closer to their grandchildren. He died there at ninety, in early 2014, and his obituary justifiably praises him. In Nakamura's last years, President Barack Obama signed a bill that added the Presidential Medal of Freedom to the many honors George Nakamura earned in a long, productive and cosmopolitan lifetime.[101] After his father's death, Gary Nakamura visited the Arroyo Grande cemetery with his father's ashes. It was April—the same month when, in 1942, the buses had stood waiting in the high school parking lot—when Gary's dad came home.

Arroyo Grande was more than 6,500 miles away from Mao's mountain headquarters, but the war was never distant. Sometimes, it fell out of the sky. In 1943, a P-39 Aircobra fighter "came in extremely low and fast" over Arroyo Grande, according to the *San Luis Obispo Telegram-Tribune*. The plane was in trouble and would crash in Shell Beach, "making a crater 15 by 20 feet and six feet deep" and scattering plane parts for one hundred yards around. The young army air force pilot, killed in the crash, was not identified. The next year, another victim was Lieutenant Isaac F. Helms, based at the Santa Maria airfield. Helms lost his life when his P-38 Lightning crashed near Oceano in an explosion felt three miles away.

So after Pearl Harbor, the curtain between home and war was thin, and Arroyo Grande became part of the war effort. Newell Strother's *Herald-Recorder* suggests that the response came fairly quickly. By January 2, 1942, ten blackout wardens had been appointed. Marine John Loomis's memory

A column of Sherman tanks from the 710th Tank Battalion on Highway 101, just south of Arroyo Grande, returning to Camp San Luis Obispo from Camp Cooke (today's Vandenberg Air Force Base). *Courtesy of the National World War II Museum, Maurice T. White Collection.*

of them was unpleasant, as they enforced blackouts with a lot of bluster and bellowing. They enjoyed their duties, Loomis felt, a bit too much. "They were mean hombres," Loomis remembered.[102] In March, the American Legion organized a home guard made up of three hundred men between thirty-five and forty-five for "police and auxiliary duties," and they began weekly close-order drills. (San Luis Obispo had formed a similar guard in 1898, after the declaration of war on Spain, but the *San Luis Obispo Telegram* likewise seemed to enjoy its own reporting a bit too much, suggesting the threat of Spanish privateers off the county's coast.)[103]

The real soldiers, of course, weren't far away. Camp San Luis Obispo hosted several army divisions during the war, thousands of young men who saw action in New Guinea, the Aleutians, the Philippines and in western Europe. The Santa Maria P-38 base meant that formations of the fast fighters would've been commonplace, and farther south, Camp Cooke—today, Vandenberg Air Force Base—specialized in armored training. Thus, columns of Sherman M1 tanks rolling through town along

Arroyo Grande Elementary School students celebrate a successful war bond drive with an officer at Camp San Luis Obispo, 1944. *Courtesy the National World War II Museum, Maurice T. White Collection.*

the two-lane Highway 101 as they headed for maneuvers with the infantry at Camp San Luis would've been fairly commonplace, as well. Local women, led by high school teacher Ruth Paulding, would serve breakfast to these young men at a recreational camp in Pismo Beach for the duration of the war. A class from the elementary school visited the camp in 1944 for a little ceremony to honor their participation in a war bond drive.

Some of them might have had mothers or elder sisters who had joined another kind of army. This one, modeled on similar organizations in World War I Britain and America, was formed in 1943 as labor shortages began to make themselves felt. On July 22, 1943, a cadre of captains, including "Mrs. George Grief, Mrs. J. Vard Loomis, Mrs. H.L. Graham, Mrs. Martha Evans, Mrs. Byron Evans, Mrs. Louise Ralph, Mrs. Jane R. Thompson and Mrs. McCallister," was formed to mobilize local women for farm work in a "Women's Land Army." The effort was heartfelt, but it wasn't enough. Ten months later, a meeting of a dozen farmers at city hall led to the call for Mexican laborers. Farther south, Nipomo farmers predicted that 1,800 workers would be needed to bring in the pea crop. As a result, the face of agricultural labor underwent a dramatic shift as Arroyo Grande participated in the *bracero* program. Mexican nationals began to make up the bulk of farmworkers in the valley.

As the war's first full year ended, *Herald-Recorder* editor Newell Strother proudly listed the valley's achievements in a New Year's 1943 edition. Among them:

- 330 young men and women in the military. Nine local boys joined the Navy in one week alone. Five servicemen had already left behind Gold Star mothers.
- Nearly $250,000 in war bonds purchases
- The collection of thirty-five tons of rubber and more than two hundred tons of scrap metal
- The sewing of 260 garments by the Red Cross
- The issuing of the war's first ration books, for sugar, in May
- The arrest in February of four "enemy aliens" and, in April, "the evacuation of 1,386 Japanese, both American citizens and foreign born."[104]

It is certainly possible to read too much into editor Strother's choice of words for the last item, but many editors would have left everything out after the word "Japanese." Strother was not among those who had clamored for the evacuation—in the weeks after Pearl Harbor, the paper's columns had called for an attitude of restraint toward local Japanese and had praised the community for its citizenship. Strother had later followed the government line but had not surpassed it in the news and editorial coverage of the evacuation itself.

By New Year's 1943, Juzo Ikeda and his son Kaz had joined his family at the Gila River, Arizona camp. Their journey there had been circuitous, and for Kaz, in his interactions with bureaucracies, it had bordered on the absurd. But for several months in 1942, after the buses had taken their friends and family away, the two Ikedas remained in Arroyo Grande.

Juzo was paralyzed, critically injured in an accident with his draft horses. (Horses would remain a feature of local agriculture even after the war, until improvements in farm machinery permitted working taller crops without damaging them.) There were no facilities for him at Tulare, not when his friends and neighbors lived in animal stalls. He was permitted to stay behind with one caretaker. It was Kaz, both because he was the eldest and because he was bilingual; Mrs. Ikeda, like many Issei, still spoke Japanese almost exclusively. When a place had been made ready, Juzo and his son were to be evacuated, as well, in the name of national security and, the government would have said, for their own protection, although Kaz, like other local Nisei remembering the postwar months, felt very little hostility from the people of the Arroyo Grande Valley.

The permit that allowed the Ikedas to stay behind essentially made Kaz a prisoner within the valley. His travel was restricted to a three-mile circle that included his father's bedside, his father's fields and the home that Vard and Gladys Loomis had opened to him. Vard, the coach of the Japanese baseball team, and his family remained faithful to their prewar friends, an attitude that was not universally popular locally, especially by those whose racism had been validated by Pearl Harbor. Some of them, Kaz was later told, came into the E.C. Loomis store and threatened to stop doing business there so long as Vard put "that Jap" up in his home.

For two and a half months, Kaz watched over both his father's land and babysat the Loomis's daughter, Sandy. Gladys, a dignified woman who was a teacher and counselor for decades at the high school and accompanied the baseball team on its away trips all over California, was incensed when sheriff's deputies searched their home for short-wave radios and outraged when she asked Kaz to give a young woman, Barbara Hall—the future wife of farmer George Shannon—a lift home, only to discover that police had pulled the couple over. A young Japanese man with a young Caucasian woman evidently threatened to disturb the peace.

A second encounter with the county sheriff came about because of a bureaucratic catch-22. A woman from the War Relocation Authority called Kaz. She had the papers that would allow him to move his father once hospital equipment and care could be arranged inland, but she could not deliver them. She asked Kaz if he could meet her at the San Luis Obispo train station, about twenty-five minutes north. Kaz agreed. However, this meant he would travel far beyond the three-mile radius permitted him.

He was on 101 northbound when he picked up a tail: two military policemen in their jeep. They had evidently radioed ahead, and when Kaz came to San Luis Obispo, sheriff's deputies took him to the county jail to await interrogation by an officer from Camp San Luis Obispo. Kaz seems to have taken this, yet another humiliation, in stride. He chatted amiably with the deputies while the WRA woman continued her train journey unaware of the trouble her good intentions had caused. Later that day, he was released.[105]

The Ikeda family eventually reunited at the Gila River camp—officially, the "Rivers Camp"—about thirty miles southeast of Phoenix. Kaz and his two brothers, Saburo and Seirin, arrived first, followed by their mother, Sei, and Juzo, whose transit required special care. Gila River had welcomed the first internees from Arroyo Grande during a month—August 1942—when the temperature exceeded 109 degrees on twenty days.

Gila River was divided into two subcamps. Butte, the larger, had 821 buildings, 627 of them residential barracks. The Ikeda family stayed in Canal Camp, with 232 barracks, because the camp hospital was nearby. Kaz remembered that his family stayed in a block of 12 to 14 barracks, each subdivided into four small apartments with a common bath facilities in the center.

Another Arroyo Grande internee, Haruo Hayashi, remembers Gila River's heat, which hit like a hammer-blow. Families would order swamp coolers from the Sears catalogue, which did little to help.[106] One father dug a basement beneath the barracks floor so that his family could find a little respite in a dark place that was at least a little cooler. What Kaz remembered was the dust. The desert winds generated terrific dust storms that hid the sun, and the dust, sharp and gritty, permeated everything: bedding; nostrils and ears; the floors of the barracks, which required endless cycles of sweeping; and even the internees' food. The dust would begin to kill older people, as well, who were susceptible to the valley fever, the lung disease that came with the hot desert winds.[107]

When Kaz formed a baseball team made up of players from Santa Barbara to San Luis Obispo, the dust destroyed his best efforts. Most of his players were Buddhist, and as their grandparents or parents began to die, many from the complications of valley fever, the sons observed the traditional forty-nine days of mourning and prayer. As a result, Kaz lost his first-string pitcher and then a catcher. Juzo then told Kaz that when he died, he had permission to go ahead and play the following week. Gila River would later produce one of the best baseball teams in the camp system, organized by a famed player, Ken Zemimura, but by that time, Kaz, like George Nakamura, had left the desert.[108]

The camp was designed for ten thousand occupants but would house fourteen thousand; internees were forced to sleep in latrines and on cafeteria tables. While the extremes of the climate—desert nights could get bitterly cold—dominated their waking hours, flies, rattlesnakes and scorpions added to the misery of a place that could not be more unlike the Arroyo Grande Valley.[109] Haruo Hayashi maintained a tenuous connection to home: he

Butte Camp, Gila River Internment Center. *National Archives.*

continued to exchange letters with his high school friends Don Gullickson, John Loomis and Gordon Bennett—the young men who would later fight the Japanese in the war's final year.

As they had at Tulare, the internees quickly got to work. Sei and Kaz cared for Juzo in shifts, feeding him, shaving him and turning him regularly to prevent bedsores. Kaz got a job as a sanitary inspector, and Haruo washed dishes for sixteen dollars a month. The young Nisei played baseball and basketball, the Issei, like Kaz's mother, Sei, found one distinct advantage to camp life: with little else to do, the elder generation that had devoted itself to hard work suddenly found time for hobbies. Sei learned flower arranging and took classes in traditional Japanese singing. For Sei's peers, Gila River brought them closer together and closer to their heritage in Kyushu, which would soon come under attack from American carrier-based airplanes.

The world just beyond the barbed wire must have seemed almost as hostile. Rumors began to spread that the internees were insufficiently patriotic and that they were being coddled—in fact, the food in the camps, some said, was far better than the wartime rations permitted the general population. But one friend the Japanese had was First Lady Eleanor Roosevelt. When her husband had issued Executive Order 9066, she was outraged; the woman he'd relied on to be his chief ambassador and intelligence-gatherer for the

Eleanor Roosevelt, bitterly opposed to her husband's Executive Order 9066, visits Gila River in 1943 with War Relocation Authority director Dillon Myer. *National Archives.*

New Deal now found, on this issue, that the lines of communication were cut. Roosevelt refused to discuss 9066. But she would persist in asking to visit a camp. Eventually, she wore the administration's resistance down. She came to Gila River in April 1943 and won the hearts of the internees there with a subtle gesture. She'd heard the rumors about the food in the camp. It was a hot day, so she asked for a glass of milk. She took a sip, handed it back and said, quite distinctly, "It's sour."[110]

The Japanese faced internment at Gila River with what seemed to be inexhaustible patience. This was a common characteristic among internees, a stoicism marked by the phrase *shigata ga nai*, literally translating to "it can't be helped," which describes a tendency to cooperate in order to make the best of a bad situation. It does not imply surrender or meekness. Ben Dohi was fourteen when he and his family were evacuated, and he remembered, fifty years later, how angry he was.[111] Kaz recalled a visit by army personnel to the Gila River camp. They had come to solicit signatures to a loyalty oath and to solicit recruits, as well. Kaz signed the loyalty oath reluctantly because it required him to serve in the military if

Shigechika and Kimi Kobara at Gila River with their children (left to right): Iso, Towru and Namiko. *Photo courtesy the Cal Poly Re/Collecting Project and the Fuchiwaki and Sanbonmatsu families.*

required. He did so only after a long talk with his dying father, who urged his son to remember how good America had been to them. Kaz never considered himself anything other than a loyal American, but he resented the hypocrisy of being recruited by the government that had so mistreated his friends and family.[112]

Like the Ikedas, the Kobara family, who would play a pivotal role when the camps began to close in 1945, endured by keeping themselves busy. Shigechika continued to farm on some of the camp's seventeen thousand acres—melons did particularly well—and he at least had the satisfaction of growing the vegetables that his block shared at mealtimes. But the Kobaras found that most young people did not share their ability to sustain life in the desert. They were impatient, restless and acutely aware of the enormity of what had been done to them—a point made manifest by barbed wire and the armed guard in the camp tower. Shigechika's wife, Kimi, recalled that "the young generation, in particular, did not want to stay in the camp any longer, so they left for Chicago and Ohio. In the end, many of those left in the camp were older people and children."[113]

Younger people got out in different ways. Ben Dohi went to school in Missouri. Haruo Hayashi joined the army and trained with the 442nd Regimental Combat Team in Mississippi as the war wound down. (Here, he

Bill Agawa of Arroyo Grande (right) at work on an Illinois farm. Many Nisei got out of the camp by joining the army or by finding jobs in the Midwest and mountain states. *Courtesy the Bancroft Library, University of California at Berkeley.*

encountered a new kind of racism. When the Nisei recruits reached Camp Shelby, they needed to use the bathroom. Which one? They tried "Colored" but were angrily chased out by black GIs and rounded on by a white sergeant who told them to never pull a stunt like that again. Haruo, bewildered, found that he was a white man, according to the arcane etiquette of Jim Crow.)[114]

Bill Agawa worked in Illinois wheat fields; Kaz Ikeda topped sugar beets in Idaho and Utah.

The young people who escaped may have saved themselves in ways they couldn't have foreseen. Kaz lived to be ninety-four. Haruo, who lost Rose, his remarkable, generous-hearted wife, in the summer of 2015, still lives on the Hayashi farm. Several of his sons are successful farmers, as well, though two took a different path: they became prominent local surgeons who are known for both their skill and their compassion. Ben Dohi lives on land now farmed by his two sons. Getting out may have been key to their long lives because many internees lost their health as well as their freedom. A 1997 study revealed that internees had a rate of a cardiovascular disease twice that of the Japanese Americans who lived in the interior and so escaped internment. Many of them experienced the symptoms of post-traumatic stress syndrome, including flashbacks.

The impact of the camps extended into the third generation, or Sansei, whose parents commonly refused to discuss the camps with their children, and this contributed to a family dynamic fraught with tension and with shame. In some families, the Sansei felt intense pressure to assimilate, which, in turn, generated a sense of emptiness, a loss of cultural identity and an even more intense pressure to succeed in school and beyond—which most of them did.[115]

Juzo Ikeda's life had been a successful one, marked by hard work. But his workplace had been beautiful—green hillsides, fields of black earth and, in the distance, shimmering white sand dunes. He could smell the sea. When Juzo had counseled Kaz to sign the loyalty oath, it was out of gratitude, for he could savor the kind of freedom, in short pauses with his horses when he reached the end of a row of crops, that comes with self-sacrifice and dedication. Japan had destroyed his family's fortunes and so had trapped those who stayed behind; in coming to America, Juzo had set himself and his sons free.

But when death came for him in 1943, Juzo was in a makeshift hospital in a barren desert camp. He died not long after asking his son to remain loyal to the nation that had made them prisoners.

CHAPTER 7

THE PACIFIC WAR

Letters from 'Our Boys'" in the *Arroyo Grande Herald-Recorder* included a wry masterpiece from a sailor named Felix Estibal, serving in the South Pacific, published on October 9, 1942. Felix was writing to his foreman, Javier Pantaleon, at the Waller-Franklin Seed Company in the Arroyo Grande Valley, where he worked before the war. It captures both the relentless monotony of navy life and a wonderful sense of humor that helped one sailor to endure it:

Dear Pan:

I hear the boatswain's mate passing a rumor that mail will leave in the near future, so I will include a brief report on myself. I am filled with good intentions to write you more often, but am fuller of good excuses.

During the rare occasions when the weather is bad, I don't write on account of the bad weather. When it is fair, the hot sun enhances my natural inclinations to be lazy and sleepy. My eight hours a day on watch add the finishing touches. I watch mostly for the little men who aren't there, but the Captain insists that they may be there any time. Anyway when [the members of the crew of his ship, the *Walke*, her named struck out by the censor] *see them then they won't be there long.*

Notwithstanding all this I frequently get out my papers and pen and drape my elbows over a mess table in a threatening manner. I think of you and wonder what you're doing. I reflect that this is a big wet ocean, and

Marines from the Fifth Division—which included an Arroyo Grande private, Louis Brown—under fire on their Iwo Jima landing beach, February 28, 1945. *U.S. Marine Corps photo.*

that we've been at sea so long that the salt is caking in my hair, that this business about mermaids is a lot of baloney, that seeing the world would be nicer if it wasn't all water, that mail and Christmas come with about the same frequency, and that the war will [be] over in six months to 10 years.

I day dream about shore liberty in a good old U.S.A. port where there are a hundred pretty girls to one sailor, nothing costs over a dime, and me with three months' pay on the books. Oh Boy!

About that time my literary efforts are interrupted by that leather-lunged whistle blower, the boatswains' mate, yelling that it's time for drill, battle stations, chow, target practice, movies, inspection, field day, air bedding, sweep down, peel spuds, scrub decks, fuel ship, carry stores, dump garbage, darken ship, pump bilges, blow tubes, pipe down, relieve the watch, or what have you.

Whereupon I sheath my pen and go to work, eat or sleep, as the case may be, without having written a word to you. It may be just as well, as the censor would probably have cropped them out anyway.

The Navy is a great life alright [sic]. *I'm getting so used to living with 200 men in enough space for two that when I get out I can use a telephone booth for a house and lot. However, it could be worse. We have good weather, good chow, good health, good guns, good digestion, good appetites, and may Heaven forgive that leather lunged whistle blower, the boatswain's mate.*

While I can't exactly say I'm having a good time and wish you were here, I hope you are well and wish I was there. In the meantime, don't worry about me as I can take good care of myself and the other guys and I'm doing all right. At least I'm well and O.K.

Say Hello to all of your friends and the most to you.

FELIX[116]

When this letter appeared, Mess Attendant Third Class Felix Estibal had five weeks to live.

In the segregated navy of World War II, Estibal was a steward—a servant—and that was the only rating to which Filipino Americans and African Americans could aspire. While black troops faced incredible discrimination in the wartime army, as well, they at least were given a chance to serve in combat units.

When combat came to Estibal and *Walke*, the results were tragic. Shortly after his letter was published, Felix died on November 15, 1942, in one of the horrific naval battles for Guadalcanal when a Japanese Long Lance torpedo—deadly and accurate, unlike the defective American torpedoes used early in the war—hit the *Walke*. Its bow was blown away, and Felix and over eighty of his shipmates died; many of them escaped the initial explosion only to be killed in the water by the concussions from the *Walke*'s depth charges as they detonated in plummeting to the seabed.[117]

Two weeks after *Walke* was lost, the *Arroyo Grande Herald-Recorder* reported the loss of another local sailor, a young man who grew up in nearby Nipomo and joined the navy to make it a career. Donald S. Runels was a lifer promoted from the ranks—a "mustang" in the language of the World War II navy—and as an ensign in his thirties, he would play his part in the fight for Guadalcanal. The Runels family was an important part, meanwhile, of Arroyo Grande life. One cousin, Tom, would grow up to become a civic-minded farmer—a sense of duty seems to mark the family—and two-term city councilman.

But the first Runels to see action in the Pacific War was Donald's eight-year-old son, Jim.

Felix Estibal's ship, the destroyer *Walke*. *U.S. Naval Institute.*

In an interview with a Medford, Oregon newspaper in 2011, Jim vividly remembered the attack on Pearl Harbor. Japanese fighters and torpedo planes flew close overhead as he watched the ships on Battleship Row burn. His vantage point for the attack infuriated his mother, Mae, who climbed up onto the roof of the Runels family home and dragged little Jim to safety. His father's ship, the heavy cruiser *Northampton*, was out to sea with Admiral William F. Halsey's carrier task force. When it returned to Pearl Harbor the next day, Jim recalled that his father was furious. Years before, the *Northampton* had paid a ceremonial visit to Japan. Now, Donald grabbed his little collection of Japanese souvenirs and threw them into the fireplace.[118]

Ensign Runels was soon in the thick of the Pacific War as the "Noras," the men of the *Northampton*, were part of the task force that shielded USS *Hornet* as it launched James Doolittle's army air force bombers in the raid on Tokyo in April 1942. The cruiser provided escort and antiaircraft support for the carrier *Enterprise* in the war's first turning point, the Battle of Midway, in June 1942 and reunited with the *Hornet* in October, taking the doomed carrier, hit repeatedly by Japanese dive bombers and torpedo planes at the Battle of Santa Cruz, under tow.

Northampton, the cruiser on which Donald Runels served, enters Pearl Harbor, December 8, 1941. *Courtesy Naval Historical Center.*

The attempt had to be abandoned, and *Hornet* had to be scuttled. The *Northampton*'s luck ran out the following month, on November 30, during the Battle of Tassafaronga. The lethal agent of its destruction was the same that had blown the *Walke* apart: the Long Lance torpedo. The Japanese excelled in night battles, and it was in a brief, vicious nighttime battle that the *Northampton*, along with the three American cruisers ahead of it in battle line, was hit.[119] Two torpedoes struck *Northampton* in the engine room and stern, and the explosion that followed was so violent that men at their bridge stations on the nearby light cruiser *Honolulu* reacted immediately. They burst into tears.[120]

The *Northampton* lost power. Dead and helpless, its crew powerless to stop the flooding, it sank four hours later, taking fifty-five crew members, including Runels, with it. The Noras would miss their ship, and they would miss their comparatively elderly ensign, who hadn't forgotten what it was like to be an enlisted man.

"I've heard stories from those who served with my dad on the *Northampton* about how he performed as an officer, about how they thought the world of him," Jim Runels told a newspaper reporter. "He was the kind of guy everybody liked."[121]

Runels's comrades thought so much of him that a destroyer escort was named for him; Jim and his mother attended the christening in Orange, Texas, in August 1943.[122] Jim rode the ship named for his father down the stays and into the Gulf of Mexico as it was launched. *Runels* saw service in the Mediterranean before its transfer to the Pacific for picket duty—one of the most dangerous naval assignments there was during the Okinawa kamikaze campaign. An inexperienced Japanese pilot, on his first and last combat mission, saw, in his mind's eye, a ship like the little *Runels* as a heavy cruiser or a battleship, and so the picket vessels were lost in great numbers.[123]

So the South County lost two young men, and the navy took a terrible beating; however, it was men like Estibal and Runels who had so disrupted Japanese naval operations in the Solomons that they were prevented from reinforcing Guadalcanal. They, and the soldiers and marines fighting so hard to secure the island, helped to make it, along with the Battle of Midway, an early turning point in the Pacific War.

If Guadalcanal was a turning point, Tarawa was one of the most costly teaching moments of the American war, and it led to two close encounters with history for a brother and sister from the lower Arroyo Grande Valley, from the little town of Oceano. This is where the farm fields end at steep seaside sand dunes and where the packing sheds and the loading docks sit alongside railroad tracks that carry valley produce to distant markets.

The brother was a marine private, George Murray, who was killed in action in the Battle of Tarawa in the Gilbert Islands in November 1943. It was a horrific battle—one of the best accounts of it comes in an aptly titled book, *One Square Mile of Hell.* Since Tarawa was the first objective in Admiral Chester Nimitz's Central Pacific campaign, many mistakes were made that would save the lives of later marines and of the GIs who landed on the coast of Normandy seven months later.

One of the mistakes in this pioneering amphibious assault was in the miscalculation of the tides at Betio Island, the key objective in the Tarawa Atoll. The tides shifted capriciously and so left many of the marines unable to land on D-day, November 20, because their landing craft, the Higgins boat, was unable to surmount the coral reef that guarded the approach to Betio's landing beaches.

George Murray was among the marines stranded outside the reef in the shallow-draft, flat-bottomed Higgins boat, essentially a ship-to-shore shuttle and so miserably unseaworthy. While earlier units took intense fire—2,200

A Higgins boat carries marines toward Betio during the Battle of Tarawa. After the first wave, these landing craft, because of unpredictable tides, were unable to surmount the coral reef; George Murray and his comrades would have to wait to go in. *U.S. Marine Corps photo.*

of the 5,000 marines in the initial wave were killed or wounded—his unit, the First Battalion, Second Marine Regiment, spent most of D-day circling, hour after hour, impotent. It must have been maddening for them, and they were hungry, wet, seasick and terrified.

It was close to 10:00 p.m. when Murray's company was finally ordered to land in support of the first waves, desperately clinging to a sliver of beach below a sea wall and flanking a pier on Betio. The marines had to transfer from their landing craft—the Higgins boat would prove essential to the war effort, but this day was a hindrance—to LVT's, the smaller amphibious tractors that also were facing their first test under fire. Murray's company hit the beach at about 11:30 p.m.[124]

A Department of Defense summary prepared for Murray's descendants is both colorless and oddly moving in its description of what happened at that moment:

Marines enjoy a rare moment of rest at Tarawa. A beached amphibious tractor, like the one that carried George Murray ashore, provides some cover. *U.S. Marine Corps.*

> *Three tractors of Company B landed on the left side of Red Beach Two. When the men tried to disembark from the first two tractors, only nine of the twenty-four men actually reached the beach…Private First Class Murray's Casualty Card indicates that he died of gunshot wounds to the head and chest on 20 November 1943. Private First Class Murray was reported buried in East Division Cemetery…Row A, Grave 6. Based on PFC Murray's recorded circumstances of death and the indication that he was initially buried at this location, it seems likely that PFC Murray did make it to the beach before being killed.*[125]

PFC Murray didn't make it home. His remains have since been lost. Local historian and museum curator Linda Austin has joined Murray's nephew and namesake, George Winslett, in a long and emotionally charged search, lobbying the Defense Department and winning the support of JPAC—the Joint POW/MIA Accounting Command—in the search for Murray. In a tragedy of errors, navy SEABEE teams reorganized and reconfigured East

Division Cemetery after the battle; after the war, Army Graves Registration teams, guided by information from Marine Corps chaplains present for the original burials, could not find the cemetery. After digging several cross trenches, the team finally began to find graves—but only 129 of the more than 400 they'd expected. Several sets of remains were transferred to Hawaii for identification, but Murray was not found, either on Betio or in the forensic labs on Oahu. For his mother, Edith, it was like losing her only son twice. She now had no formal way to honor him, and she was heartbroken.[126]

So was Murray's sister, Thelma. She wasn't willing to wait to honor her younger brother—they were just two years apart—so she, too, joined the marines. She became a driver—and a good one—stationed at Camp Lejeune, North Carolina. Thelma eventually married another good driver, a truck driver, Elmer Thomas Anderson, with whom she'd hitched a ride from home in Oceano to a new duty post in San Francisco. Anderson drove for what would become Certified Freight Lines, located where the Bank of America now stands on Branch Street. An honorably discharged army air force staff sergeant, Elmer would sometimes debate good-naturedly with his bride of more than forty years over who, precisely, outranked whom.[127]

One of Thelma's assignments as a driver had come when a dignitary visited Camp Lejeune on December 18, 1944, and he had to have the best marine possible to transport him. Marine Lieutenant General Herbert Lloyd Wilkerson, a Guadalcanal veteran, was an officer trainee that day. He remembered in a 1999 interview: "The black cabriolet, with its top down, pulled up close to our commanding officer, LTCOL Piper, who presented us to the Commander-In-Chief. I was in the front rank within 20 feet from the auto and could hear their voices. The auto was driven so close to the commanding officer that he hardly needed to move to reach the side of the vehicle."[128]

The driver needed to be exact, driving the car almost to the trainees' shoe tips, because the dignitary couldn't get out of the cabriolet and so reveal his paralysis to the fit young marines.

Thelma's passenger that day, of course, was President Roosevelt.[129]

The fact that FDR was the president of a nation that didn't particularly want them did nothing to cool the enthusiasm of the young Filipino men who wanted to leave the fields and the restaurant kitchens of Arroyo Grande. They wanted to fight. Their insistence on fighting with the Americans to liberate their people led to the formation of the First Filipino Infantry Battalion at Camp San Luis Obispo in the spring of 1942. This was not a unit segregated by choice or by custom—in contrast to the rigid color

Thelma and George Murray, in a composite photo made for their mother. *Courtesy Linda Austin and the Oceano Train Depot Museum.*

line drawn by the wartime navy, the army even allowed Filipino American officers, for example, to command Caucasian troops in Europe—but it was instead animated by the same kind of fierce patriotism that had made Emilio Aguinaldo's resistance fighters such powerful antagonists in the Philippine Insurrection earlier in the century.

U.S. Army trainers, selected for that duty from the Seventy-seventh Infantry Division, were astonished by the enthusiasm and the intuitive understanding of soldiering exhibited in their trainees, who adapted quickly to all the demands of military life, from maintaining the M1 Garand rifle to motor pool duty. A distinction of the First Battalion, and later the First Regiment, was its use of the bolo knife, a machete-like weapon that amateur armorers in the unit fashioned from automobile springs, and hand-to-hand combat training included *escrima*, the Filipino martial art for which the bolo knife is the mainstay.[130]

The troops were fiercely loyal, as well, to Lieutenant Colonel Robert H. Offley, their commanding officer, who had served in MacArthur's Philippine army. Within three months, his popularity would generate so many volunteers that it would lead to the formation of a second regiment at Fort Ord, under the command of Lieutenant Colonel Charles L. Clifford, and both units would undergo basic and advanced training at bases throughout the state. By the war's end, 250,000 young Filipino men had volunteered for military service.

But their status as soldiers did little to ease the discrimination they'd endured before the war, and it enraged their commanding officer. One soldier remembered an incident in northern California:

> *In Marysville we were…at Camp Beale. And one night, four of us wanted to go into town 'cause we learned there was a Chinese restaurant there. We wanted some rice, you know, Chinese food! We hadn't had any in a long time. And we just sat around, no service. So the Sergeant called over the waiter and the waiter called the manager. The manager said, "I'm sorry, Sir. We can't serve Asians." Now this was a Chinese restaurant and I guess we were startled when we heard that…And he explained that, "Hey, I'm sorry we can't serve you. There's a city ordinance that we can't serve Asians." And here we were soldiers, you know…Colonel Offley made a stand. He went to the city fathers and told them, "Hey, you serve my people, they are American soldiers, or I'll declare Martial Law on you."*[131]

There no further problems in Marysville. The soldiers began to refer to Offley as *Tatay*, meaning "Papa."

Lieutenant Colonel Offley faced another legal hurdle when the time came close for his men to ship out to the Pacific. Many of them had fallen in love—with young Caucasian women—which was somewhat inevitable. Because of the prewar immigration restrictions, Filipino men had outnumbered Filipino women by as much as one hundred to one in many

Members of the First Filipino Infantry Regiment pay a visit to the Arroyo Grande farm of Sergio Reyes. *Photo courtesy the Cal Poly Special Collections and Archives, Juliet Betita Collection.*

parts of the state, which still had rigid miscegenation laws on the books. Offley could not declare martial law on the California state legislature, but he could requisition buses. In the spring of 1944, he instituted a kind of marriage by shuttle: his men could marry legally in Gallup, New Mexico, and did, thanks to Offley's "Honeymoon Express."

That year, the *Arroyo Grande Herald-Recorder* identified at least sixteen valley Filipino Americans (in 1943, Congress had passed legislation allowing them American citizenship) fighting under MacArthur's command—first in New Guinea, where they'd had to endure another racist insult. They were employed by one general as manual labor until an enraged *generalissimo* intervened. MacArthur's fidelity to the Filipino people was genuine. One of his chief aides was the Filipino soldier-statesman General Carlos Romulo, who would someday become secretary general of the United Nations. The *Herald-Recorder* featured Romulo on its front page when he came to nearby Guadalupe to speak in April 1944.[132] During the war, he seemed tireless. He was a leader of the resistance to Japan, a war bond fundraiser and perhaps the most important recruiter for units like the First Filipino Infantry Regiment. In the fall of 1944, MacArthur made good on his promise to return when American forces came ashore at Leyte. They followed their commander, determined and dramatic, splashing through knee-deep water to mark his own personal invasion. Romulo was just behind him.

The combat record of the California Filipinos whom Romulo helped recruit was a distinguished one, including service with the Alamo Scouts, commando units that operated deep in enemy territory on New Guinea and in the Philippines. The majority of the Filipino American GIs saw their first action in Leyte and on Samar, the island where, during the Philippine Insurrection, the intemperate General Otis had ordered the killing of every Filipino over the age of ten. They would later fight with the Sixth Army in the invasion of Luzon, with the Alamo Scouts and a ranger battalion meanwhile pulling off one of the most dramatic raids of the war. In January 1945, they liberated five hundred Allied prisoners of war at Cabanatuan, including survivors of the Bataan Death March, some of whom had been anticipating retribution—execution by their captors—as American forces advanced. The "Great Raid" spared them that fate, and in February, American forces re-took Manila.[133]

A month later, an Arroyo Grande sailor and a native of Luzon, Camilo Alarcio, found himself escaping with his life while serving on an aircraft carrier off the Japanese coast.

Just as Felix Estibal had been on the doomed destroyer *Walke*, Alarcio was a mess attendant assigned to the aircraft carrier *Franklin*. He joined the ship in February 1945 in Honolulu as it returned to the war. A kamikaze attack the previous October had caused major damage that sent the ship to Bremerton, Washington, for repairs and a refit. By March 1945, the *Franklin* and its one hundred aircraft had returned to combat and were engaged in raids on Kagoshima, Kyushu—the seat of the prefecture from which most Arroyo Grande Japanese had emigrated—when the Japanese struck back on March 19.

It was a little after 7:00 a.m., with half the crew at breakfast, exhausted after repeated calls to their general quarters stations—the kamikazes had returned in great numbers—when a Japanese "Judy" bomber launched a more traditional attack. The aircraft somehow penetrated the carrier's defense screen and scored two hits with 550-pound armor-piercing bombs. More than thirty aircraft with their ordnance and fuel lines were packed on the main deck. The *Franklin* seemed likely to share the fate of four aircraft carriers of Admiral Chuichi Nagumo's Pearl Harbor striking force, which, at Midway in June 1942, American fliers had discovered and sent to the bottom in flames with their flight decks laden with bombs, gasoline lines and aircraft.

One of the bombs flipped a thirty-two-ton deck elevator like a flapjack, leaving it canted at a forty-five-degree angle in its well. The shaft below it and the decks adjacent were an inferno. Crewmen were incinerated instantly; aircraft on the hangar deck melted and plummeted to decks farther below. Twelve of the thirteen pilots in the famed Marine Corps "Black Sheep" Squadron, based, since the beginning of the year, at a naval air station near Goleta, died in their ready room.[134]

Camilo Alarcio, three decks below, felt the big ship heel from one side to the other—the explosion even shook the decks of distant ships below the *Franklin*'s horizon. Alarcio clambered up the flight deck only to realize that he was freezing. He made his way back to his quarters to fetch a jacket, flak jacket and flashlight. Back on the flight deck, he saw sailors run for their lives as the fires spread. In the heavy smoke, some ran into the turning propellers of aircraft, their engines still running for their next combat mission. Alarcio then saw the cruiser *Santa Fe* alongside, and that ship's crew began to throw lines across to the *Franklin* as the flames threatened to engulf the carrier's sailors, including Alarcio. He grabbed one of the lines and made his way across; other sailors fell and drowned, some so badly burned that they couldn't save themselves, while others were pulled under by the turning of the *Franklin*'s screws. Alarcio survived.[135]

The *Franklin*'s survival was in doubt. The initial explosion was just the beginning. As fires reached twenty more aircraft, fueled and ready for flight on the hangar deck, they perpetuated a chain reaction that, throughout the day, set off stores of bombs, rockets, antiaircraft ammunition and aviation gasoline. At one point, the violence inside the *Franklin* made the thirty-two-thousand-ton ship shudder and spun it like the needle on a compass hard to starboard, where it lay dead in the water. It then began to list ominously, heavy in the water and under the weight of the thousands of tons of water used to fight the fires.[136]

While its crew worked to stabilize the ship, the *Santa Fe* was a constant companion alongside, fighting fires and evacuating sailors while periodic explosions showered its deck with both steel and human fragments. Eventually, the *Franklin*, drifting toward Kyushu, was taken under tow, but its engineers re-lit the boilers so it could begin to make for Ulithi in the Caroline Islands for emergency repairs. The *Franklin*'s voyage did not end at Ulithi. It put in at Pearl Harbor, and then, on April 28, 1945, the "Big Ben," its scars still visible and grievous, returned home to New York Harbor and the Brooklyn Naval Yard.[137]

USS *Franklin*, March 19, 1945, in a photograph taken from the cruiser *Santa Fe*. *Naval Historical Center.*

Camilo Alarcio's name is on the next muster roll,[138] but neither he nor "Big Ben" fought again. After the war, he became the much-beloved father and grandfather of a large, vital and attractive family; his children and grandchildren made their marks in Arroyo Grande as superb athletes. A single adjective in his obituary and on his tombstone seems to summarize his character and the characters of his brothers from the *Franklin* best: "Devoted."

On another tombstone at the Arroyo Grande District Cemetery, a young marine's oval photographic portrait stares evenly back at visitors. His name was Louis Brown, and he was killed a little more than two weeks before the *Franklin*'s ordeal began, on March 1, 1945. He was an Arroyo Grande boy and was Queen Isabel's miracle. Mr. and Mrs. Antonio Brown added Louis to their family twenty years after his brother had been born, when they, immigrants from the Azores, were in their forties.

They lost him when he died on Iwo Jima two days before he turned twenty-one. His commanding officer there, General Holland Smith, had a premonition before the battle: "This will be the bloodiest fight in Marine

Above: Adored by his children and grandchildren, USS *Franklin* survivor Camilo Alarcio (front row with two younger family members) became the patriarch of an Arroyo Grande–area family that excelled in athletics, teaching and business. *Photo courtesy the Alarcio family.*

Left: Private Louis Brown's headstone, Arroyo Grande District Cemetery. *Author photo.*

Corps history," he said. "We'll catch seven kinds of hell on the beaches, and that will be just the beginning."[139]

Of course, Smith was right. Later, on Okinawa, the Japanese would let the Americans come to them. On Iwo Jima, the Japanese, commanded by an inspired tactician, Lieutenant General Tadamichi Kuribayashi, intended to make the marines pay dearly for every yard they took. Outnumbered three to one, Kuribayahsi's twenty-one thousand men weren't garrisoned on the island—they *inhabited* it and had created a rabbit-warren of caves, tunnels, machine-gun nests with interlocking fields of fire and masked mortar positions. Kuribayashi must have known he was doomed, but he sought a battle that would be remembered in history. Indeed, he had no intention of dying or of letting his men die in anonymity.

But that is how Private Louis Brown died. As a member of the Twenty-seventh Replacement Draft[140]—made up of marines with no combat experience and kept at work as stevedores on the landing beaches—he would have been fed into the battle as the marines struggled to secure the island. The replacement drafts were used to plug holes, so they were new to their units. Brown was a replacement in the elite Twenty-eighth Marine Regiment, with the men who had raised the flag on Mount Suribachi, and replacements were resented for their newness. To the veterans of the Twenty-eighth, marines like Brown were a nuisance and a distraction unless they lived long enough to become veterans themselves. In a history of the battle, marine colonel Joseph H. Alexander notes:

> *The new men, expected to replace invaluable veterans of the Pacific War, were not only new to combat, but they also were new to each other, an assortment of strangers lacking the life saving bonds of unit integrity. "They get killed the day they go into battle," said one division personnel officer in frustration. Replacement losses within the first 48 hours of combat were, in fact, appalling.*[141]

Brown died on a day when the Twenty-eighth was assaulting Hill 362 A, honeycombed with caves that proved to be death traps. At the mouth of one of them, Bill Genaust was killed. He was the Twenty-eighth Marines' motion-picture photographer and had filmed the Suribachi flag-raising, during which Genaust had warned AP still photographer Joe Rosenthal to turn around and get his shot—the one that would prove immortal. Genaust's body was never found.[142] Genaust had lived a long time for an Iwo Jima marine; Private Brown died no more than forty-eight hours after going into

Marines from the Twenty-eighth Regimental Combat advancing over broken ground typical of the terrain on Hill 362 A, where Louis Brown was killed. *Department of Defense/ U.S. Marine Corps photo.*

combat for the first time. The Navy Department listed his cause of death as "burns, entire body,"[143] the kind of ghastly wound, in this battle, that was commonly inflicted by antipersonnel mines, which Kuribayashi's men had sown by the thousands.[144] Louis Brown died the most brutal of deaths, and he died among strangers.

His parents did not want their boy to lie amid strangers, so they brought him home. His photo, in his uniform and garrison cap, is on the military tombstone that Antonio Brown ordered for his boy, for Queen Isabel's miracle.

Not all of Arroyo Grande's encounters with the distant Pacific war were such tragic ones. A local businessman, Clayton Conrow, donated a knife to one of the periodic war drives (this one included a tagline that chirped "Give your hunting knife—it may save a life!"); 6,800 miles and untold months later, the knife he donated wound up in the hands of a stunned crew member of the hospital ship *Samaritan*. The sailor showed the knife, with Clayton's named carved into the handle, to his best friend, Pharmacist's Mate Kenyon Conrow, Clayton's son.[145]

Kenyon evidently was a popular young man. Army staff sergeant Bob Little heard that his neighbor was on the *Samaritan* when it was berthed off Guam—where former high school football coach Max Belko had been killed in the earlier marine assault on the island. Little tried but failed to see Kenyon, but he at least sent a consolation letter to Clayton Conrow. Like many letters home, it compared Arroyo Grande with the world beyond:

> *I have been able to get around and see most of the island. There is quite a bit of game here, but we are not allowed to hunt, as there are so many fellows there would soon be nothing left: besides, there's the risk of shooting each other where there are so many of us.*
>
> *There are a lot of deer here. Only last night about sundown as I was coming in from work, there was a great big buck standing right in the middle of the road. He was plenty fat, but also plenty slow. A deer that slow around Arroyo Grande wouldn't last five minutes.*

A soldier like those cared for by the *Samaritan*, Private Charles Faux was incredibly chipper about his circumstances. He wrote home from India in 1944 that he "got it in the right side in June, and had malaria three times and Jungle rot. This is a nice place to have them all."

Marine private John Loomis would fight in the last major ground campaign of World War II, on Okinawa. He wrote home mid-campaign, in the spring of 1945:

> *We are back three miles from the front licking our wounds now, and waiting for I don't know what. Maybe we go back and maybe we don't. I guess I've seen most of this island so far—enough, anyway. Shuri Castle was a rich joint and Naha used to be quite a town...I had my picture taken the other day with a couple of fellows by "Division." I don't know if it will get in the papers or not. I sure didn't look like much that day.[146]*

Loomis was thin and tired, worn down by a long campaign that he couldn't have known involved his best friend and cousin from Arroyo Grande, Gordon Bennett, who was serving as a nineteen-year-old seaman in Vice-Admiral Marc Mitscher's Task Force 58, which had to endure a hail of kamikaze attacks offshore.

A marine fires a burst from his Thompson submachine gun in this iconic photograph, taken on Okinawa. *U.S. Marine Corps photo.*

The marines fought alongside U.S. Army troops that had trained not far from Arroyo Grande. The Ninety-sixth Infantry Division was based at Camp San Luis Obispo and practiced amphibious landings on the coastline just south of Morro Bay before they launched a costly attack—the battle would claim even the American commander, General Simon Bolivar Buckner—on the defensive works anchored by Shuri Castle.[147]

Loomis and Bennett came home from Okinawa and picked up their friendship—marked by a kind of Tom-and-Huck passion for outdoor adventures and practical jokes—where they'd left off. They wrote a book about their teenage years. John held Marine Corps reunions at his family's Tar Springs Ranch in the Huasna Valley, and Gordon was fond of talking to young people about life in the old days and perhaps even fonder of floating with them in a task force of inner tubes down the Salinas River. The two men—unpretentious and fiercely loyal to their hometown—picked up other prewar connections, as well, with men like Haruo Hayashi and Kazuo Ikeda, who weren't "enemy aliens" but the best of friends.

PART IV

BINDING

···

CHAPTER 8

THE GIFT OF A GENERATION

There were harbingers of the war's end in the *Arroyo Grande Herald-Recorder* long before V-J Day in the fall. The paper still had one eye on the Pacific War when it announced on May 11 the end of the war in Europe: "A.G. GIRDS FOR FINISH FIGHT AS GERMANY QUITS." The story below the headline describes a restrained celebration as businesses closed, flags appeared everywhere and an interfaith service was scheduled for the high school gym.

News still trickled in from Europe. Several local fliers were released from prison camps; in the previous week's edition, a story detailed the wounding of Sixty-ninth Division soldier Orville Schultz, who ended up losing his left hand. Schultz recognized a lieutenant from his rifle company in the famed photo of GIs greeting Soviet soldiers at the Elbe. The column "Letters from 'Our Boys'" described a visit by Private William Barker to Hitler's Berchtesgaden mountain retreat, and there were attempts by GIs to put into words the destruction wrought on Germany and the human horror of a just-liberated Buchenwald concentration camp.

In the American tradition, those who sensed the end in the keenest way were advertisers. During the summer and fall, the *Herald-Recorder*'s display ads included dancing appliances that reminded gas customers that a return to normalcy was imminent, the phone company counseled patience as it tried to keep up with the influx of orders that anticipated the peace and the

Bank of America's loan office offered visions of a middle-class home-to-be or a prosperous-looking farm (with a misplaced, midwestern corn silo) in an effort to kindle postwar business. But the most prescient of all the newspaper's ads in these months has to be one for the "great new smooth riding Thayer folding coach," just $44.50 at Ewers' Home Furnishings in Pismo Beach. It's a baby buggy.

Servicemen were returning to resume their peacetime lives. The new teacher at Branch Elementary Elementary was married to a veteran of the privations of 1942 Bataan. F.F. Smith, married to local dressmaker Lenore Smith, and his brother-in-law, S.W. Sanson, were army veterans and, in mid-1945, entrepreneurs. The newspaper noted their partnership in selling "the E.C. Livingston prefabricated all-steel building units," an enterprise in marketing the humble Quonset hut that had emerged from the incredible shift the nation made from peacetime to wartime production. In another story, Andy Wilcox, recently separated from the service at Camp Roberts, planned to open a body shop on West Branch Street.

It took longer for other fighting men. The dead began to come home from Europe in 1947.[148] Antonio Brown's son Louis, killed on Iwo Jima, was returned to Arroyo Grande in 1949. Clara Gularte's youngest son, Frank, remained in France with his comrades in a military cemetery. The family of George Murray, the marine killed on Tarawa, still hopes for his return today. The sailor Felix Estibal, who served on the destroyer *Walke* off Guadalcanal, will never return.

In the first edition of the 1945 new year, the newspaper announced, formally and stiffly—the story probably altered little from the original government press release—another kind of homecoming. Interned Japanese were permitted to return to their homes. A later story noted that businessman Vard Loomis had invited a representative from the War Relocation Authority to speak on the topic of the returnees.

The last time all of the Gularte children were together, 1944. Frank, in uniform, in front of his mother, would be killed in action in November 1944. Just above him is Manuel, who would serve as an artilleryman and survive the war. Joe and Tony, at left, would run the family farm during the war; Mrs. Clara Gularte is flanked to the right by her six daughters (from left to right): Mary, Edwina, Clara, Rose, Annie and Barbara. *Photo courtesy Annie Gularte Silva.*

No one faced a postwar world more difficult than the Japanese who returned to the valley.

Mits Fukuhara, an army veteran whose family had come to Arroyo Grande very early in the twentieth century, estimated that fewer than half the prewar families came back to the valley.[149] In May, the Kobara family was the first to return to their home—a neighbor, Joe Silveira, had farmed their land during the war. Silveira warned them that the family that had rented their home while the Kobaras were in the camp at Gila River had moved out and that they had better return in a hurry before someone burned the house down.

The War Relocation Authority encouraged the head of the family, Shigechika, to return—since he had land and a home, he represented, to the WRA, a stabilizing influence that might make the transition easier for subsequent internees—an assumption that would prove to be correct.

Anticipating trouble, two War Relocation Authority agents stayed with Shigechika, and his daughter Isoko for several weeks, their car parked out front while the family slept in the hallway, away from the windows. Iso remembered hearing distant gunshots, presumably fired in the air. Her mother, Kimi, would always be grateful for the kindness of the WRA agents who watched over her husband and daughter while she remained behind at Gila River.[150]

Those agents were doing the right thing, because hostility toward Japanese Americans remained intense, a fact that had a distinct political calculus. The Roosevelt administration had not dared announce the end of the internment program until December 1944, after the elections that would bring FDR his fourth term.

Roosevelt might have been right. An earlier announcement may well have cost him votes. Evidence that feelings still ran high came when the first West Coast internees returned. There were some sixty reported acts of terrorism, many in the San Joaquin Valley. Shots were fired into the homes of Japanese American farm families. There was an attempt in Fresno to dynamite packing sheds belonging to the Doi family. Both the Delano Buddhist temple and the town's Japanese school were burned by arsonists. Meanwhile, to the north in San Jose, drive-by gunmen opened fire as one family fled from its burning home in another arson fire.[151]

Arroyo Grande's Japanese were spared this kind of physical violence. But much damage had been done to their property while they were in Arizona. The Loomis family had set aside a dehydrator building near E.C. Loomis & Son as a makeshift warehouse for their friends when they were evacuated

The Kobara family after the war. *Left to right, top row*: Ken Kobara, Mitsuo Sanbonmatsu (Keith's father), Towru Kobara and Hilo Fuchiwaki; *middle row*: Mari Kobara (Ken's wife), Nami Kobara Sanbonmatsu, Shigechika Kobara (grandfather), Kimi Kobara (grandmother), Iso Kobara Fuchiwaki, Lori Fuchiwaki, Fumi Kobara and Joan Kobara; *bottom row*: Gary Kobara, Keith Sanbonmatsu, Dona Fuchiwaki, Susan Fuchiwaki and Steve Kobara. *Photo courtesy the Cal Poly Re/Collecting Project and Keith Sanbonmatsu.*

in 1942; the building was isolated, though, and most of the furniture stored there was vandalized or stolen by 1945.

The Loomises—especially Vard, who'd coached the prewar Nisei baseball team, and his wife, Gladys—were regarded with intense suspicion by the more virulent racists in the valley since they had provided the warehouse and watched over the farmland of the Fukuhara and Ikeda families.[152]

But the Loomises were not alone in their recognition that these were the same people who had always been and would always be their friends. Farmers like Ed Taylor and Gus Phelan loaned their returning neighbors any farm machinery they needed. Paul Wilkinson, who owned the butcher's shop in Old Arroyo, donated groceries and resumed running tabs for his Japanese customers. In fact, before the evacuation, when they had come to settle their bills with Wilkinson, he refused to accept their money. "You're going to need it," he told them.

J.J. Schnyder was a blacksmith and handyman who fixed the Kobara family's pump on Christmas Day. (On V-J Day, Strother's newspaper suggested building a swimming pool as a kind of living memorial to the young lives lost in the war, and it was Schnyder's philanthropy that made the pool a reality, as part of a new high school completed in the mid-1950s.) W.A. Baxter's service station in Pismo Beach was one of the few that not only provided service for the returnees but insisted on it. Insurance agent Pete Bachino—a Cal Poly booster who would be killed in the football team's 1960 plane crash—had cared for internees' cars and eagerly resumed his prewar business with them.[153]

Haruo Hayashi came home from the army before the rest of his family had returned from internment, and he stayed with the Bennett family, cousins to the Loomises. They told Haruo he could stay with them as long as he wanted—they took some heat for it—but soon, Haruo was able to resume his father's farming, nearly seamlessly, because Cyril Phelan and John Enos had farmed the Hayashis' land and maintained their farm equipment throughout the war.[154]

The overwhelming generosity of men like these wasn't a universal, and friendliness was not a given. Hilo Fuchiwaki was still in uniform as a member of army intelligence when he and some family members went to the movies in Pismo Beach. A patron spat on him. Shortly after, the theater manager removed the entire group, ostensibly for their own safety, which was, of course, the same excuse so frequently used to justify the internment. When the minister of the Arroyo Grande Methodist Church heard about the incident, he asked to accompany Hilo to the movies the next time he went. There were no further incidents, and the Kobara and Fuchiwaki families began attending regular services at the Methodist church.[155]

When Kimi Kobara followed her husband and daughter back from Gila River in July, the Kobara home, their workers' barracks and the Japanese school provided temporary housing for other returnees, like the Ikedas, who worked for a time for Joe Silveira, the neighbor who farmed the Kobara property during the war. Japanese families from Santa Maria found a place to stay, too, when hotels in that city refused to lodge them. With a lot of mouths to feed, Kimi went grocery shopping in Arroyo Grande, only to be told not to return. That incident sparked a turning point. Eileen Taylor, the wife of farmer Ed Taylor, was president of the Arroyo Grande Women's Club. At one meeting, she made it very clear to the membership that they had an obligation to make the returning Japanese feel welcome. Mrs. Kobara

Hilo (left) and Ben Fuchiwaki, veterans of Vard Loomis's prewar baseball team and of the U.S. Army Military Intelligence service. *Courtesy the Fuchiwaki family.*

said the atmosphere began to improve after Mrs. Taylor's speech—a speech that is, sadly, lost to history.[156]

A moment in history that is not lost, thanks to a remarkable preservation effort by Cal Poly professor Grace Yeh, is a photograph that is part of the university's Re/Collection Project—an effort to interview representatives of local immigrant groups and to copy photographs, letters and other primary source documents that are part of their heritage. One of the most extraordinary is a series of photos of a housewarming party for a returning Filipino GI, Pete Guion. It's an important occasion because Guion had broken decades of de facto segregation. He was the first Filipino American to buy a home in South County. A large group photo taken at the housewarming might be the most significant in the series, for it shows not only a proud Guion and his friends from the Filipino community but also Caucasian and Japanese faces. Something important was beginning to happen four years after the Kobara family had faced such a fearful homecoming.[157]

For Filipinos, that change came at the cost of many lives. They had fought for the country of their birth as well as the country that had showed them little good will, and finally, they began to achieve a measure of justice. Filipino veterans were given a path to citizenship—ten thousand would

Pete Guion's housewarming party. *Courtesy the Cal Poly Special Collections and Archives and Juliet Betita.*

become naturalized citizens, and under the December 1945 War Brides Act, they finally got the chance to marry and start families in America. So what followed the war was another remarkable campaign in the Philippines. This one was led by ardent bachelors, many of them former soldiers, and its objective was conquest of a different sort, in the form of a flurry of marriage proposals. Between 1945 and 1964, over four thousand Filipinas accepted and came to live in America.

Many of the men, because of immigration restrictions and anti-miscegenation laws, had deferred marriage and so were considerably older than their fiancées, and they were in a hurry to resume their lives in California. So they sought to win family approval, get a proper church wedding and arrange for the return of their new wives as quickly as possible. One local woman, Josie Bolivar, remembered her marriage as "kind of a shock" because it violated so many Filipino proprieties—parental negotiation, a protracted and tightly chaperoned courtship and the customary time it took to establish a bond between the groom and the bride's family. Her father, at first, was upset, but Josie's wedding—she was, after all, going to become an American—turned out to be a huge affair, complete with uninvited guests and feasting that lasted for days.

Perfecto Betita moved with similar speed in courting Evelyn: "Right away, he said that we didn't have much time, that they were looking for someone to marry, and it's gonna be quick, because we have to go back. After about a month's time, I found out he had already talked to my grandmother and grandfather, and my uncle and aunt. He told me he didn't have any more time to stay in the Philippines, and he wanted to…well, marry me."

The marriage was concluded, and Perfecto brought his bride to the States. When they arrived in San Francisco in July, the first thing the new husband had to do was to buy his wife a coat. She was freezing in what passed for a San Francisco summer. They took a Greyhound bus south to Arroyo Grande, where Evelyn had a reaction very similar to that of Kimi Kobara when she had come to the valley with her husband, Shigechika, in 1920. Her account is marked by the wonderful sense of humor that her children inherited:

> *Oh, we were so shocked when we came here. We thought we would come here and live in a big two-story, three-story house. But they worked at the farm, and we were shocked! We said, "This is where they live? I thought you lived in some three-story house? It's all muddy and farmy." We had to clean and scrub because, well, they're single, and they worked long days, early to late, they have no time to clean the house.*[158]

So the men and women who had their lives interrupted and changed irrevocably with the attack on Pearl Harbor would start over—or, in the case of Perfecto and Evelyn Betita, start new lives—with the war's end. Farming would still sustain the valley with families like the Hayashis, the Gulartes and the Betitas, but now the hard work and the energy of those who came home would be focused on the lives of their children.

My father was a newcomer to the valley. We would move to Arroyo Grande in 1952, when I was a baby, from Taft, but his experience was reflective of those who had lived here for generations. He, too, was an army veteran—he'd been a Quartermaster Corps officer in Europe—and he had found a position as comptroller for the Madonna Construction Company in San Luis Obispo.

Robert Gregory assumed his peers' innate sense of obligation to serve the community. In 1958, he and my mother were delegates representing St. Barnabas Episcopal Church to the Grace Cathedral convention that met to elect a new bishop, the charismatic, media-savvy James Pike. His background in banking and finance also led him to membership in the group of men who would found Mid-State Bank, now Rabobank, in 1961, and the same year, as clerk of the Branch Elementary School Board, he put together the bond issue that doubled the size of the school, expanding it from a two-room 1888 schoolhouse to a four-room post-Sputnik version.

Schools, in fact, were being built all over the South County during the 1950s and 1960s. Harloe, Shell Beach, Ocean View, North Oceano are just a few examples. The high school that Clarence Ballagh and Elliott Whitlock,

Lieutenant Robert W. Gregory, my father, 1944. *Author's collection.*

Postwar progress: The new Valley Road campus of the high school. The walnut trees, which became infested by insect pests, are now gone. *Courtesy Randy Spoeneman.*

Haruo Hayashi and Kazuo Ikeda and Frank and Manuel Gularte had attended was torn down, after fifty-five years, in 1961. A new campus, on Valley Road, had meanwhile begun classes in the mid-1950s.

The parents of the World War II generation supported the Boy Scouts, Campfire Girls and 4-H, but most of all, they supported youth sports. One of the most active Arroyo Grande boosters was Vard Loomis's catcher. Kaz Ikeda had played for the high school team, Loomis's Arroyo Grande Growers, and Cal Poly. At Gila River, where outfielders had to contend with rattlesnakes, he'd played ball behind barbed wire. Ikeda, along with his brothers, Saburo and Seirin, and a cousin, Haruo Hayashi, was instrumental in organizing local Little Leagues and Babe Ruth leagues. POVE, the Pismo-Oceano Vegetable Exchange, the Japanese American farmers' co-op, provided both funding and coaching talent for the ballplayers of the generation that arrived in such staggering numbers after the war. Sab Ikeda's players still remember, fifty years later, what a well-coached team they were—and they remember, too, a coach who wore a perpetual smile.

Coach Saburo Ikeda and his Little League team, about 1965. *Courtesy Marty Childers.*

When Vard Loomis's catcher and lifelong friend Kaz Ikeda died at age ninety-four in 2013, hundreds attended his funeral. At his graveside, they sang "Take Me Out to the Ballgame."[159]

The war that had so wounded Ikeda and his classmates, had so divided his hometown and had taken so many young lives was increasingly becoming a distant memory, lost except in history books for most of those who gathered to pay their respects that day. Kaz, like many of his peers who'd spent time in the camps, may not have forgotten the war, but he had conquered the hurt it had brought to his friends and family. He had to. In 1945, the year of his homecoming, there'd been no time for bitterness, not with so much work to be done.

That work ethic is reflected even in the one postwar extravagance Kaz allowed himself. In the early 1960s, he built his growing family, including a son named Vard, a home atop a hill off Branch Mill Road. From there, he could see the patchwork of Ikeda farm fields where, in 1837, Francis Branch had begun to clear the tangled *monte*. A century later, four generations of the family from Kagoshima had planted the richest crop the valley has ever known.

One indication of Kaz Ikeda's importance to Arroyo Grande is his image on this mural—on the building that once housed the market owned by the family of B-17 copilot Elliott Whitlock—completed by Visalia artist Colleen Mitchell-Veyna in 2014. Ikeda is shown with a vegetable crate with the POVE (Pismo-Oceano Vegetable Exchange) label. This was the Japanese American growers' co-op, formed in the 1920s and still in operation today. *Author photo.*

NOTES

CHAPTER 1

1. "The Dust Bowl in New Mexico," *Santa Fe Journal*, santafejournal.blogspot. com/2009/05/dust-bowl-in-new-mexico.htm.

2. Graham Robb, *The Discovery of France: A Historical Geography from the Revolution to the First World War* (New York: Norton, 2007).

3. "Domingo Martinez," Genealogy, Family Trees & Family History Records at Ancestry.com, http://ancestry.com.

4. "35thinfantrydivision-memory.com," 35thinfantrydivision-memory.com.

5. Air Force Association, "The 367th Fighter Squadron," by Edward S. Chickering, in *Air Force Fifty* (Paducah, KY: Turner Pub, 1998), 79.

6. Ira Wyche, "Cherbourg," in *The Cross of Lorraine: A Combat History of the 79th Infantry Division, June 1942–December 1945*, http://digicom.bpl.lib.me.us/ww_reg_his/39.

7. John C. McManus, *The Americans at Normandy: The Summer of 1944—The American War from the Normandy Beaches to Falaise* (New York: Forge, 2004), 160.

8. Paul Huard, "The MG42 Machine Gun Was Hitler's Buzz Saw—War Is Boring—Medium," https://medium.com/war-is-boring/the-mg42-machine-gun-was-hitlers-buzz-saw-aaebfde958e4.

9. Sterling Wood, "History of the 313th Infantry," *World War Regimental Histories*, vol. 39 (Washington, D.C.: Infantry Journal Press, 1947) 80–81.

10. "Company C Morning Report, 313th Infantry Division, 15 July 1944," National Personnel Records Center, Archival Programs Division, St. Louis, MO.

CHAPTER 2

11. "Hawken Rifle," Wikipedia, https://en.wikipedia.org/wiki/Hawken_rifle.

12. Robert A. Brown, *Story of the Arroyo Grande Creek* (Arroyo Grande, CA: South County Historical Society, 2002).

13. "Francis Ziba Branch," FamiliesHeadingWest.com, http://familiesheadingwest. com/people-2/branch-francis-ziba.

14. "Neighboring Rancheros," DanaAdobe.org, www.danaadobe.org/neighboring-rancheros.

15. Wallace Ohles, "The Murders in the Old Mission," Mission San Miguel, California website, http://www.missionsanmiguel.com/history/reedfamily.html.

16. "Exciting Scene in San Luis Obispo—Another Outlaw Hung," *New York Times*, October 29, 1853, http://query.nytimes.com/gst/abstract.html?res=9501E3DF103AE334BC4151DFB7678388649FDE.

17. "Pacific Coast Railway," Wikipedia, https://en.wikipedia.org/wiki/Pacific_Coast_Railway.

18. Cynthia Lambert and Carol Roberts, "Vigilante Justice in Arroyo Grande » Photos from the Vault," David Middlecamp, http://sloblogs.thetribunenews.com/slovault/2011/01/vigilante-justice-in-arroyo-grande.

19. Madge C. Ditmas, *According to Madge: Early Times in South San Luis Obispo County and the Arroyo Grande Valley* (Arroyo Grande, CA: South County Historical Society, 1983).

20. Brown, *Arroyo Grande Creek.*

21. "David Newsom," from C.M. Gidney, Benjamin Brooks and Edwin M. Sheridan, *History of Santa Barbara, San Luis Obispo and Ventura Counties, California* (Chicago, IL: Lewis Pub. Co, 1917), http://www.rootsweb.ancestry.com/~cagha/biographies/n/newsom-david.txt.

22. "Ramon Branch" from "Experience El Rincón Adobe History," Talley Vineyards, https://www.talleyvineyards.com/Experience-Talley-Vineyards/El-Rincn-Adobe-History.

23. Gary Hoving, "Arroyo Grande Police Department History," City of Arroyo Grande, http://www.arroyogrande.org/266/Department-History.

24. Jean Hubbard, "The First United Methodist Church of Arroyo Grande Celebrates 125 Years of Ministry," First United Methodist Church of Arroyo Grande, CA, http://www.worshipweekly.com/125th.htm.

25. Ruth Paulding, *The Gallant Lady* (Arroyo Grande, CA.: Hubbard Printing, 1984).

26. Ella Honeycutt, "Arroyo Grande Valley Farmland History," Arroyo Grande Valley Harvest Festival, www.agharvestfestival.com/arroyograndevalley.htm.

CHAPTER 3

27. Merry E. Wiesner, *Discovering the Global Past: A Look at the Evidence*, vol. 2 (Princeton, NJ, 2007).

28. "Azoreans and Madeirans," Minority Rights Group International—Working to Secure the Rights of Minorities and Indigenous Peoples, http://www.minorityrights.org/1820/portugal/azorea.

29. Robert Pavlik, "Shore Whaling at San Simeon Bay," *History in San Luis Obispo County*, http://www.historyinslocounty.org/Shore%20Whaling%20by%20Pavlik.htm.

30. *Yesterday, Today, and Tomorrow*, vol. 5 (Arroyo Grande, CA: South County Historical Society, 1981–89).

31. "Antone Brown," Ancestry.com, http://person.ancestry.com/tree/46359583/person/6524617140/facts.

32. "Frank Rosa Gularte," Family Trees, Ancestry.com, http://person.ancestry.com/tree/47225128/person/24.

33. Sucheng Chan, "European and Asian Immigration into the United States, 1820s to the 1920s," in *Immigration Reconsidered: History, Sociology, and Politics*, edited by Virginia Yans-McLaughlin (New York: Oxford University Press, 1990), 47–49.

34. Cherstin M. Lyon, "Alien Land Laws," *Densho Encyclopedia*, http://encyclopedia.densho.org/Alien_land_laws.

35. Ella Honeycutt, "Arroyo Grande Valley Farmland History," Arroyo Grande Valley Harvest Festival, www.agharvestfestival.com/arroyograndevalley.htm.

36. Shigechika and Kimi Kobara, interview by Yoshiko Tachibana, Oral History Program, California Polytechnic State University, San Luis Obispo, March 1, 1980.

37. "California, Passenger and Crew Lists, 1882–1959," Ancestry.com, http://search.ancestry.com/search/db.aspx?dbid=79.

38. "Joseph Vard Loomis—A Silent Hero," https://familytreelove.wordpress.com/2014/10/29/joseph-vard-loomis-a-silent-hero.

39. General James Rusling, "Interview with President William McKinley," *Christian Advocate*, January 22, 1903.

40. Alvitah Akiboh, "The 'Massacre' and the Aftermath: Remembering Balangiga and the American War in the Philippines," *U.S. History Scene*, http://ushistoryscene.com/article/balangiga.

41. "American Soldiers in the Philippines Write Home About the War," *History Matters: The U.S. Survey Course on the Web*, http://historymatters.gmu.edu/d/58.

42. Ibid.

43. Grace Yeh, "Routes and Roots: Cultivating Filipino American History on the Central Coast," https://sites.google.com/site/centralcoastroutesandroots.

44. John Robison, "Afrin Fernando and Benny Goodwell," photograph and recollection published in *Arroyo Grande Memories*, Facebook.com, https://www.facebook.com/photo.php?fbid=10202457880047005&set=gm.1036760786340548&type=1&permPage=1.

45. Douglas P. Jentzen, "Growing Conflict: Agriculture, Innovation, and Immigration in San Luis Obispo County 1837–1937" (master's thesis, California Polytechnic State University–San Luis Obispo, March 2011), http://digitalcommons.calpoly.edu/theses/460.

CHAPTER 4

46. *San Luis Obispo Tribune*, "A Talented Musician, His Life Cut Short," author column, December 6, 2010, http://www.sanluisobispo.com/2010/12/06/1398084/viewpoint-a-talented-musician.html.

47. *Arroyo Grande Herald-Recorder*, "Wayne Morgan, Arroyo Grande Youth, Is Killed in Pearl Harbor Attack," December 26, 1941.

48. Pauline Ellis Scruggs, "Jack Leo Scruggs," USSArizona.org, http://www.ussarizona.org/website/stories/uss-ariz.

49. Theodore C. Mason, *Battleship Sailor* (Annapolis, MD: Naval Institute Press, 1982).

50. Molly Kent, "USS *Arizona*'s Last Band: The History of U.S. Navy Band Number 22," http://www.ussarizonaslastband.com.

51. U.S. Navy, "USS *Arizona*, Report of Pearl Harbor Attack," Naval History and Heritage Command, http://www.history.navy.mil/research/archives/digi.

52. Ellis Scruggs, "Jack Leo Scruggs."

53. Jean Hubbard, "The First United Methodist Church of Arroyo Grande Celebrates 125 Years of Ministry," First United Methodist Church of Arroyo Grande, CA, http://www.worshipweekly.com/125th.htm.

54. Will Tarwater, personal correspondence with author via Facebook, August 2014.

55. David Middlecamp, "Pearl Harbor Attack, Japan Opens War on U.S. World War II Week by Week," Photos from the Vault, *San Luis Obispo Tribune*, December 2011. http://sloblogs.thetribunenews.com/slovault/2011/12/pearl-harbor-attack-japan-opens-war-on-u-s-world-war-ii-week-by-week.

56. Tarwater, personal correspondence.

57. Kobara and Kobara, interview.

58. Kazuo Ikeda, interview by Ricardo Medina, Oral History Program, California Polytechnic State University, San Luis Obispo, January 8, 1980.

59. Haruo Hayashi, personal interview, Arroyo Grande, CA, June 20, 2015.

60. Effie McDermott, personal correspondence with author via Facebook, June 19, 2015.

61. Donald J. Young, "Japanese Submarines Prowl the U.S. Pacific Coastline in 1941," *World War II*, July 1998, http://www.historynet.com/japanese-submarines-prowl-the-us-pacific-coastline-in-1941.htm.

62. *Atascadero News*, "Atascadero People Awakened by Sound of Torpedoed Tanker," December 26, 1941.

63. "Correspondence Regarding January 1942 Broadcasts [John B. Hughes]," Japanese American Evacuation and Resettlement: A Digital Archive, Bancroft Library, University of California–Berkeley, http://vm133.lib.berkeley.edu.

64. Lynne Olson, *Those Angry Days: Roosevelt, Lindbergh, and America's Fight Over World War II, 1939–1941* (New York: Random House, 2013), 179–80.

65. University of Denver, "Decision to Evacuate," https://www.du.edu/behindbarbedwire/decision_to_evacuate.html.

66. Pat Nagano, "Japanese Relocation and Evacuation on the Central Coast in 1942," Morro Bay for Oldtimers, http://www.oldmorrobay.com/nagano.html.

67. Ikeda, interview.

68. "Japanese American Evacuation Cases," LegalDictionary.com, http://legal-dictionary.thLeTTTefreedictionary.com.

69. Department of Justice, Civil Division, *Arroyo Grande Valley Japanese Growers Association*, 1952 (Los Angeles, CA: National Archives Administration, 1957).

70. Cynthia Lambert, "Two Teens Arrested in Alleged Arson of Boy Scout Building," *San Luis Obispo Tribune* and SanLuisObispo.com, May 9, 2011, http://www.sanluisobispo.com/2011/05/09/1594561/two-arrests-made-in-fire-that.html.

Chapter 5

71. Loren Ballagh, "Letter to Researcher Peter Connon: Clarence Ballagh," Ancestry.com, July 14, 1986, http://trees.ancestry.com/tree/7516801/person/-107.

72. "Pathfinders and Night Missions," 482nd Bomber Group, http://www.482nd.org/night-missions.

73. Allan Palmer, MD, "Survey of Battle Casualties, Eighth Air Force, June, July, and August 1944," chap. 9 in *Medical Department, United States Army: Wound Ballistics*, edited by James Boyd Coates Jr., MC (Washington, D.C.: Office of the Surgeon General, Department of the Army, 1962), http://history.amedd.army.mil/booksdocs/wwii/woundblstcs/chapter9.htm.

74. "B-17 41-9051 'Flaming Mayme [*sic*],'" Military Aircraft Crash Sites, http://militaryaircraftcrashsites.blogspot.com/2013/05/b-17-41-9051-flaming-mayme.html.

75. "413th Bomb Squadron," American Air Museum in Britain, http://www.americanairmuseum.com/unit/1042.

76. Elliott Whitlock, "Letters Home from 'Our Boys' on His 24th Mission," *Arroyo Grande Herald-Recorder*, April 7, 1944.

77. "B-17 42-97524," American Air Museum in Britain, http://www.americanairmuseum.com/aircraft/10599.

78. Barrett Tillman, "Ploesti—The Rest of the Story," History Net: Where History Comes Alive—World & US History Online, http://www.historynet.com/ploesti-the-rest-of-the-story.htm.

79. 376th Heavy Bombardment Group, http://www.armyaircorps-376bg.com.

80. Jess Milo McChesney's Army Air Corps career, from flight school through discharge, is revealed among several shorts on Arroyo Grande men in the service from the *Arroyo Grande Herald-Recorder*, 1943–45.

81. Nancy Shore, "From the Atlantic to the Pacific: Amelia Earhart, Woman of Achievement," Facts On File History Database Center, 1987, http://www.fofweb.com/History/Main.

82. "Sadami Fujita," Ancestry.com, http://search.ancestry.com.

83. Franklin Odo, "100th Infantry Battalion," *Densho Encyclopedia*, http://encyclopedia.densho.org/100th%20Infantry%20Battalion.

84. J. Herzig, "The Battle of Bruyeres and the Rescue of the 'Lost Battalion,'" Stand Where They Fought: My Tour to Battlesites of WWII, http://standwheretheyfought.jimdo.com.

85. "The Battle of Bruyeres—'Lost Battalion,'" 442nd Regimental Combat Team Historical Society, http://www.the442.org/battlehistory/vosges.html.

86. Duane Vachon, "Japanese Minds, American Hearts—442nd Regimental Combat Team, U.S. Army, WWII," *Hawaii Reporter*, August 11, 2013, http://www.hawaiireporter.com/japanese-minds-american-hearts-442nd-regimental-combat-team-u-s-army-wwii/123.

87. *Arroyo Grande Herald-Recorder*, "Letters from 'Our Boys,'" 1943–45.

88. Raymond Gantter, *Roll Me Over: An Infantryman's World War II* (New York: Presidio Press, 1997).

89. Rick Atkinson, *The Guns at Last Light: The War in Western Europe, 1944–1945* (New York: Henry Holt and Co., 2013), 164–70.

90. Patrick Sullivan, "War Story: Russ Kunz, 94, Is Finally Talking About WWII Combat," *Port Townsend & Jefferson County Leader*, November 6, 2013, http://www.ptleader.com/news/war-story-russ-kunz-is-finally-talking-about-wwii-combat/article.

91. "Tank Busters: The History of the 607th Tank Destroyer Battalion in Combat on the Western Front," http://www.scribd.com/doc/83666584/Tank-Busters-The-History-of-the-607th-Tank-Destroyer-Battalion-in-Combat-on-the-Western-Front#scribd.

92. "A Special Tribute" to World War II and other veterans, South County Historical Society, http://www.southcountyhistory.org/ww11vets/ww11.html.

93. *Arroyo Grande Herald-Recorder*, "Frank Gularte Dies in Action," December 15, 1944.

94. Hugh M. Cole, "The First Attacks on St. Vith," in *The Ardennes: Battle of the Bulge* (Washington, D.C.: Office of the Chief of Military History, Dept. of the Army, 1965).

95. "Youmans [*sic*] is with 101st Airborne Troops," *Arroyo Grande Herald-Recorder*, March 30, 1945. Youman's birthday and background are from Ancestry.com.

96. David Middlecamp, "Two Arroyo Grande Men Killed in Action: Photos from the Vault," *San Luis Obispo Tribune*, October 13, 2014, http://www.sanluisobispo.com/2014/10/13/3294539_two-arroyo-grande-men-killed-in.html?rh=1

97. Dick Winters and Cole C. Kingseed, *Beyond Band of Brothers: The War Memoirs of Major Dick Winters*, Google Books, https://books.google.com/books.

CHAPTER 6

98. *Tulare News*, Fresno State Digitized Collections, 1942, http://cdmweb.lib.csufresno.edu/cdm.

99. Correspondence with Fuchiwaki family, February–May 2014.

100. "George Nakamura," JACL, http://hirasaki.net/Family_Stories/Nakamura.htm.

101. George Nakamura Obituary, HoustonChronicle.com, January 26, 2014, http://www.legacy.com/obituaries/houstonchronicle/obituary.aspx?pid=169278121.

102. Bee Hodges, "Supporting Japanese-Americans During the Internment [Excerpt]," *Heritage Press*, South County Historical Society, August 2007.

103. Wilmar Tognazzini, "One Hundred Years Ago: 1898," http://wntog.tripod.com/98.html.

104. *Arroyo Grande Herald-Recorder*, January 1, 1943.

105. Ikeda, interview.

106. Hayashi, interview.

107. Ikeda, interview.

108. Kazuo Ikeda, interview by Ken Kenyon, *Moebius* 8, no. 1 (2010), http://digitalcommons.calpoly.edu/moebius/vol8/iss1/15.

109. Karen Leong, "Gila River," *Densho Encyclopedia*, http://encyclopedia.densho.org/Gila%20River.

110. Ibid.

111. Ben Dohi, "Enduring Values: The Living Story of a Japanese-American Farming Community," interview by Erin Phillips, *California Civil Liberties Program*, December 3, 2008.

112. Ikeda, interview.

113. Kobara and Kobara, interview.

114. Hayashi, interview.

115. "Children of the Camps: Health Impact," PBS: Public Broadcasting Service, http://www.pbs.org/childofcamp/history/health.html.

CHAPTER 7

116. Felix Estibal, "Letters from 'Our Boys,'" *Arroyo Grande Herald-Recorder*, October 9, 1942.

117. David H. Lippman, "Second Naval Battle of Guadalcanal: Turning Point in the Pacific War," History Net, November 1997, http://www.historynet.com/second-naval-battle-of-guadalcanal-turning-point-in-the-pacific-war.htm.

118. Paul Fattig, "A Child of Pearl Harbor," *Medford (OR) Mail Tribune*, December 7, 2011.

119. "USS *Northampton*," Military History Encyclopedia on the Web, http://www.historyofwar.org/articles/weapons_USS_Northampton_CA26.htm.

120. John Toland, *The Rising Sun: The Decline and Fall of the Japanese Empire, 1936–1945* (New York: Random House, 1970).

121. Fattig, "Child of Pearl Harbor."

122. *Arroyo Grande Valley Herald-Recorder*, "Escort Vessel Will Bear Name of Nipomo Hero," August 6, 1943.

123. Robert L. Gandt and John Pruden, *The Twilight Warriors* (Old Saybrook, CT: Tantor Media, 2010).

124. John F Wukovits, *One Square Mile of Hell: The Battle for Tarawa* (New York: NAL Caliber, 2006).

125. *George Murray*, Department of Defense, Joint POW/MIA Accounting Command, 2011.

126. April Charlton, "Family Waiting for WWII Soldier's Return from Tarawa," *Santa Maria Times*, May 28, 2011, http://santamariatimes.com/news/local/family-waiting-for-wwii-soldier-s-return-from-tarawa/article.

127. Donald Anderson and Rosemary Anderson, "Thelma Murray Anderson," e-mail to author, August 14, 2014.

128. "Maj. Gen. Herbert Lloyd Wilkerson," interview by L.J. Kimball September 20, 1999.

129. *Arroyo Grande Herald-Recorder*, "Thelma [Murray] Glenn Drives FDR's Car," January 12, 1945.

130. Alex Fabros, "The Boogie-Woogie Boys," *Positively Filipino*, http://www.positivelyfilipino.com/magazine/the-boogie-woogie-boys.

131. Dean Aleagado and Linda A. Revilla, "History, Heroes and Untold Triumphs: Filipino-Americans and World War II," California State University–Sacramento, http://www.csus.edu/aas/filipinos/viewers%20guide/1.htm.

132. *Arroyo Grande Herald-Recorder*, "Romulo Urges Large Audience, Recall Bataan—Keep Fighting," April 21, 1944.

133. Alex Fabros, "California and Second World War: California's Filipino Infantry," California State Military Museum, http://californiamilitaryhistory.org/Filipino.html.

134. David Lippman, "USS *Franklin*: Struck by a Japanese Dive Bomber During World War II," History Net, March 1995, http://www.historynet.com/uss-franklin-struck-by-a-japanese-dive-bomber-during-world-war-ii.htm.

135. Camilo Alarcio, interview by Yvonne Caldon, video, 2004.

136. Joseph A Springer, *Inferno: The Epic Life and Death Struggle of the USS* Franklin *in World War II* (Minneapolis, MN: Zenith Press, 2011).

137. Lippman, "USS *Franklin*."

138. "Camilo Serraon Alarcio," USS *Franklin* muster roll, April 30, 1945, Ancestry.com.

139. Sergeant Christopher Zahn, "Echoes of Iwo Jima Heard by Present-day Marines," *Quantico Sentry Online*, http://www.quanticosentryonline.com.

140. Antonio Brown, "Headstone Applications for Military Veterans," Ancestry.com.

141. Zahn, "Echoes of Iwo Jima."

142. Jim Gregory, "Saving Private Brown," *SLO Journal Plus*, June 2009.

143. "Certificate of Death," Private Louis Brown, Bureau of Medicine and Surgery, Navy Department, Washington, D.C., June 1945.

144. Robert E. Allen, *The First Battalion of the 28ᵗʰ Marines on Iwo Jima: A Day-by-Day History*, 200.

145. *Arroyo Grande Herald-Recorder*, February 5, 1943.

146. Ibid., "Letters from 'Our Boys,'" 1943–45.

147. Daniel Krieger and Jim Gregory, "Rehearsal at Montana De Oro, Times Past," *San Luis Obispo Tribune*, November 9, 2012.

Chapter 8

148. Antonio Brown, "Headstone Applications for Military Veterans," Ancestry.com.

149. Mits Fukuhara, "Enduring Values: The Living Story of a Japanese-American Farming Community California," interview by Danielle Johnson, *California Civil Liberties Public Education Program*, February 13, 2009.

150. Hodges, "Supporting Japanese-Americans."

151. "Return to the West Coast," *Densho Encyclopedia*, http://encyclopedia.densho.org/Return_to_West_Coast.

152. "Joseph Vard Loomis—A Silent Hero."

153. Hodges, "Supporting Japanese-Americans."

154. Hayashi, interview.

155. Correspondence with Fuchiwaki family, February–May 2014.

156. Kobara and Kobara, interview.

157. "Housewarming Party for Pete Guion," Re/Collecting Project, California Polytechnic State University–San Luis Obispo, from the Juliet Betita Collection, http://reco.calpoly.edu/items/show/1582.

158. Josie Bolivar and Evelyn Betita, interview by Kevin Doria; Kristen Anton, "Routes and Roots: Cultivating Filipino American History on the Central Coast," https://sites.google.com/site/centralcoastroutesandroots/roots/filipina-women-arrive/coming-to-the-us.

159. Kenneth Klein, "Community Remembers 'Kaz,'" *Santa Maria Times*, February 17, 2013, http://santamariatimes.com/news/local/community-remembers-kaz/article_c134e2ee-78d6-11e2-a67d-001a4bcf887a.html.

INDEX

ABOUT THE AUTHOR

Jim Gregory taught American literature, modern world literature, cultural anthropology, advanced placement U.S. history and AP European history for thirty years at Mission College Preparatory School in San Luis Obispo, California, and at Arroyo Grande High School. He, with his brother and two sisters, was raised in the Upper Arroyo Grande Valley and attended the two-room Branch Elementary School. He then studied journalism and history at Cuesta College; the University of Missouri–Columbia, where he received his bachelor's degree; and California Polytechnic State University–San Luis Obispo. He was an editor at ABC-Clio in Santa Barbara and a newspaper reporter in San Luis Obispo before becoming a teacher. He was the Lucia Mar Unified School District's Teacher of the Year in 2010–11. In 2004, he received a Gilder-Lehrman Fellowship to study the Depression and New Deal with Pulitzer Prize–winning Stanford University professor David Kennedy, an experience that only deepened his fascination with the 1930s and 1940s. He has led several student trips to Europe, including visits to many of the villages and cities where young Americans fought in 1944–45. He recently taught a class on descriptive writing for young people as part of the Central Coast Writers Conference in San Luis Obispo. Jim is married to Elizabeth, a teacher and campus minister at St. Joseph High School in Santa Maria, and the father of two sons, John and Thomas. The Gregory family shares increasingly precious space in their Arroyo Grande home with one Basset hound, two Irish setters, one tortoise and a small army of cats.

Visit us at
www.historypress.net
···
This title is also available as an e-book